S0-BZI-182

Edward Babson and his fiancée, Jennifer Capizzi, attended a friend's wedding on the day of Edward's untimely death.

Sail Away

An adventurous journey
around the world
toward healing

From the Journals of

Don & Lois Babson

Credits

The cover photograph of *Que Sera Sera* was
taken by Sandra Hollingsworth
of Scotland from the yacht *Vegawind.*

The photograph of Edward and Jennifer
was taken by Kristen Campagnuolo
of Westbury, New York.

The photograph taken at the Holy Sepulchre
and the world map are printed with
the permission of Jimmy Cornell,
author, friend and organizer of
the Millennium Odyssey Rally.

The poem, "Sail On", is printed with
the permission of dear friend,
Joette McDonald, poet.

For Further Information Contact

Lois and Don Babson
PH: 419/357-0776
or 419/602-0998

www.DonBabson.com

ISBN: 978-0-692-00008-3

Printed by RS • 3911 Venice Road • Sandusky, OH • 44870

In memory of our eldest son, Edward,
without his loss we would never have had
the need to run away to the sea
to escape our grief.
Sometimes what appears to be
lost is found,
venturing into the unknown
on a journey of faith.

Acknowledgements

We are so grateful to all those that made our trip so fantastic! At the top of the list must be Gayland and Mary Louise Lehman. These sea faring friends took us aboard their fine 43 foot yacht, *Wandering Star*, to sail upon the deep blue seas of the Atlantic. Here then they proceeded to give us our first lesson in survival at sea. They took us fifty miles offshore on the edge of a tropical storm in huge boarding seas. We did survive. If one can sail in those conditions for three days, one can sail anywhere, or so we thought.

Our sincere thanks to our management team: Fred Babson, president; Kevin Coghlan and John Balliette who provided the leadership to the staff of Babson Fluid Power Inc. Our gratitude to that staff, who did a fine job keeping our company running smoothly. We never doubted your abilities!

A huge thank you to our daughter, Deonne who put us up at her home each time we flew back to Ohio. We loved being with your family. And thanks also for letting us spend time with our eight-year-old grandson, Nathan, for ten weeks sailing from Tonga to Australia. Thanks as well to Nate for crewing and teaching us how to win at cards! He won all of the time so maybe he taught us how to lose at cards.

Our gratitude goes to our daughter–in-law, Shelly, who picked up our mail and paid our bills in a timely manner and to Evan and Bunny Evans who helped us get *Que Sera Sera* south to Florida and gave us much advice.

Thanks to Dan and Karen Somes of Vero Beach who found us a great safe dock in the marina at Grand Harbor.

We must thank Fred and Shelly Babson who helped us sail from Florida to Bermuda safely, it was not easy.

And also Julia and Carol Papcke who bid us a bon voyage from St. Augustine, and then welcomed us to Rome.

Thank you, Ann Harsh and Ralph Nehrig of *Harmonie* for your friendship before the trip, and throughout the rally.

We are grateful to Jimmy Cornell and his staff at World Cruising Club, especially, John Ellis who looked after us throughout the entire rally.

We certainly appreciated the Morgans, Lou, Jacky, L.J. and Zetty from Oconomowoc, Wisconsin, who took us under wing, and looked after us for the first half of the journey to Australia. It was a sad day when all the Morgans and Ralph and Ann left us to sail around the Cape of Good Hope.

Here's to good friends Teva & Hinano of *Prinz Karl,* to Christ and Ern of *Pimalo,* and to the many other rally members that we grew to love. Charles and Saundra Gray became like a brother and a sister to us, and were always ready to do some adventuring to the unknown. They are gracious, generous and loving people.

Thanks also to those who crewed legs: Ken Watt, Dan Somes, Bill and Marlene Noyes, Hank Stein, Julie Papcke, Tom and Frank Silva, and Joe and Joette McDonald.

Thanks to Joette for her poem and other sisterly guidance. A big thank you also goes to Dr. Jackie Justice and Pam Leszynski for proof reading. We are also grateful to Sue Stiegelmeier for her graphic design skills.

A sincere thank you goes to Deborah Schisler, friend, neighbor and president of Pabodie Design Studio who came to our rescue in the last hour in order to make our deadline.

It is impossible to express what our editor and desktop publisher, Sandy Rider, has done to make this book become what it is. Without her help and guidance this book would never have been put together. So, Sandy, our heartfelt gratitude to you.

Just as it takes two to sail our boat it has taken two to live this story. I am so very blessed to have my wife, Lois, of 51 years, still at my side as a lifetime partner and loving crew. Together we created this wondrous around the world adventure!

PREFACE

I have always kept a complete logbook each day on all of our sailing voyages. I fill them up with technical data such as weather, wind strength, course steered, and every four hours, day and night, with latitude and longitude positions taken from one of our three GPS instruments. Yet I had never written any kind of story.

That all changed after our visit to Sri Lanka. This two-week saga was so unbelievable that I had to write it all down.

Thanks to our laptop PC I could hunt and peck away to my heart's content. I certainly had time because we were traveling along at five miles an hour day after day for four and half years.

We went through three PCs before getting back to Ohio. One PC was splashed by a wave one night. Two days later it started to smoke so I quickly threw it overboard. An undiscovered leak in the bow allowed water to seep in by the navigation station destroying two other computers.

The joy of writing seemed to grow with each story written. Soon I began to feel like I was missing something unless I was writing about the life that we were living out on the oceans of the world. I wrote for several hours each day whenever possible.

I believe that the act of writing filled my mind with positive thoughts, and helped to push out some of the pain that resulted from our son Ed's loss.

Also Lois spent many hours arranging pictures and adding commentary in numerous photo albums so that others could enjoy the photos, and we would have our thoughts and feelings down on paper.

On returning home we put the best photos into a Power Point presentation, and Lois began to give talks for numerous organizations. After each talk the same question was asked over and over. They wanted to know if we were writing a book.

We thought we had a book armchair sailors would enjoy. After talking with our dear friend, Joette McDonald who had a lovely book of poems published, she recommended we consult with her editor. When we met with Sandy Rider, she felt our story was a lot more than a good sail-around-the-world adventure. She recommended we start adding our story of loss and healing to the book.

We hope that by sharing our story it will help others who have experienced loss, and also it will provide enjoyment for fellow sailors, adventurers, and those that wish to live life to the fullest.

1

Sail Away

We entered the outer bay of New York harbor before dawn. It was as black as the ace of spades as we felt our way up the bay with the aid of our GPS, and the numerous channel markers, to Great Kills harbor on Staten Island.

At the Great Kills Yacht Club, we discovered a group of sailors preparing to join the *Sail America* event to honor the lives lost in the trade center attack. We promptly agreed to join the fleet of 1,000 sailboats parading up the Hudson River to the city, past the World Trade Center's remaining buildings, to the George Washington Bridge.

With much anticipation, we cut two big eagle shapes from black sailcloth, and attached them to the mainsail along with large U.S.A. letters of red and blue.

Six days after arriving at Great Kills, we joined close to 100 other sailboats from the harbor, and headed up river to join the ever-growing fleet. Hundreds of boats from all of the many marinas all began to merge together under the Verrazano Narrows Bridge. Soon the river seemed to be a mass of slowly moving white triangles. Our sails, with their bold emblems, found space in the river of white. We headed to lower Manhattan, and then on past the empty space that had been the twin towers.

Not far from Manhattan is Nassau County, the place where Lois and I sustained an even larger, personal loss. That is where our son, Eddie, was taken away from us by a young woman driving drunk. This has become a day filled with sadness. Sadness for all of those innocent people who had been taken away needlessly from their loved ones, and sadness for the loss of our son.

At the George Washington Bridge, the fleet of over 1,000 sailboats turned back down river to their many marinas. We, however, continued on up the Hudson River with our heads swirling with thoughts of our recently concluded big ocean adventure. For four and a half years we sailed across three of the oceans of the world, one of them three times. Our long voyage had been an odyssey in the classical sense. Lois and I had been literally on a quest to reclaim our lives after sustaining the unbearable loss of our son.

In 1996 we made the life-changing decision to join the Millennium Odyssey Canarias Rally, not as a noble voyage of exploration and not to be the first to finish the race for fame. Our decision was motivated by the need to escape. It was escape from our grief—the grief that we had both been living with for over a year after the death of our eldest son, Edward Scot Babson

Ed, 32, had just graduated from New York Institute of Technology, and was managing and opening TGI Friday restaurants in the New Jersey area. He was 22 days from being married to a wonderful woman when he was killed by a drunk driver on Long Island, New York. Eddie and his fiancée, Jennifer Capizzi, had just attended a co-worker's wedding when Deana Yakkey lost control of her car on a winding road 50 feet from the new bride's house.

A photograph taken that fateful day shows our fun-loving Eddie sporting a big grin, his arm around Jennifer, and a cigar tucked behind his ear—on top of the world.

Eddie and Jennifer had planned to be married three weeks later on the beach near our home in Ohio. Our house, on the shores of Lake Erie, had been the base camp for summer water fun when our kids were growing up. Sailing was a big part of our family life. Our kids always said, "You sure better like your brother and sister because when you are out on the boat, there is no one else to play with." Maybe it was fitting that we received the news of Eddie's death on our sailboat.

Lois remembers that day, June 8, 1996: "Our daughter was celebrating her wedding anniversary so we agreed to take our two and four-year-old grandsons with us sailing. It was the first time Nathan steered our boat by himself. Don and the two boys were howling at the moon to celebrate. We spent the night anchored off of Johnson Island enjoying the stars and full moon, counting our many blessings."

"All that suddenly changed when we saw our son and daughter, with their spouses, approaching on a stranger's boat early the next morning," Lois continues. "There was no question that something tragic had happened. There, still at anchor behind Johnson Island in the dreary, foggy morning mists, they told us of our son Eddie's death."

"In shock, we immediately made arrangements to fly to New York. As we were driving to the airport, I opened my Bible looking for some consolation. It just happened to open to a passage that affirmed that all those who believe in Christ will go to heaven. There was no question in our minds. We knew that our Eddie went directly to heaven," Lois states.

In the days and months to follow, Lois and I were going through the motions of living, but not really aware that life still continued outside of our grief. Our loving daughter, Deonne, plus our youngest son, Fred, were both suffering from the tragic loss of their brother. We all tried to support one another, but often being together meant too many painful memories, and the subsequent sadness of a shared loss.

Our grief rendered us unable to function or contribute much to anything or anyone around us. Both of us were extremely close to our son whose love for life spilled over to everyone he met. We each grieved his death differently.

Lois recalls, "Crying at every meal. We couldn't even eat. The first Easter after Eddie's death there was such a hole in our lives we couldn't sit around home. We went bowling in Sandusky. Can you imagine bowling on Easter? We couldn't do the same things we had done before with Eddie not there."

I was angry. I was mad at God. It was a miserable, miserable time. I was looking for someone to blame. Even our marriage was strained. I was on edge. Nothing was happy, only deep sadness prevailed.

Now into this land of spiritual limbo came a call from a sailor friend, Hank Stein, who was living in England. He told me of the World Cruising Company's latest round-the-world rally. He quickly faxed me the information. With the details in hand, our life was about to change. Making the decision to join the Millennium Odyssey Rally gave us something besides loss as our focus.

As a member of the 50-yacht-fleet sailing in this world circumnavigation event, we would carry a message of peace symbolized by the glowing flame in our individual lanterns to all the corners of the globe. The fleet would interact with people in 40 countries, and reach all the continents including Antarctica. We would be commemorating the start of the new millennium and the continuation of our journey through the stages of grief.

A rally participant could choose to start in 1998 from Israel or from London, England; Williamshaven, Germany; the Canary Islands or later from Florida. We chose to start in London because that fleet was scheduled to sail south around the two great capes of the world—Cape of Good Hope and Cape Horn. We wanted to sail to South America, and the Beagle Channel of Tierra del Fuego, Chile even if it meant that we first had to cross the North Atlantic to do so.

We had twice before crossed the Atlantic on a friend's sailboat in 1992, so even though we would be on our own smaller boat, a Hans Christian 40, we were confident that we could do it again.

During the winter of 1996 we worked hard to prepare our stout little *Que Sera Sera* for the trip. We spent a large sum of money on new equipment, for our ship was eight years old, and not equipped for extended ocean sailing. We installed: a small diesel motor with a big 200-AMP hour generator on its output shaft, plus a high-pressure water pump to make fresh drinking water, new high grade heavy duty six-volt batteries, a new hot water heater, radar, an Inmarsat C Internet-only satellite communications system, an electric autopilot, a single sideband radio, new anchor chain, all new sails, a high powered emergency position finder beacon, a life raft and numerous other safety items. Plus, for my galley cook, a new propane stove and oven. A good ship must have good victuals aboard. The necessary equipment was ordered and installed before we departed Sandusky, Ohio.

We had fixed our minds on doing this voyage, so we poured all of our spare time and finances into the preparation. During that year, I buried myself in getting the boat ready.

The tragic reality of Eddie's death was now part of our lives as we navigated a maze of anger and confusion, pain, and loss. Adding to our sadness, the insurance company requested an explanation of why Ed should be worthy of the full insurance award. I was murderous about writing it. Yet it was very easy to put together a four-page letter proving the value of his life, yet to be lived, and describing the kind of responsible person that he really was. Didn't they know that he had just finished first in his class at NYIT? Why would I have to prove my son's worth? Why should any parent have to prove that their child, killed by a drunk driver, was priceless!

Coincidentally, though, the insurance settlement, when divided four ways between Ed's immediate family, totaled $21,000 each. Lois' and my share was exactly the amount we needed to retrofit our boat for our voyage. I couldn't help but think this was Ed's last gift to us.

Six months after Eddie's death, Lois and I faced yet another challenge. Lois was diagnosed with breast cancer. After a successful lumpectomy, Lois consulted with her oncologist. He asked her if there had been a stressful event in her life recently possibly lowering her resistance, and triggering the cancer. Stressful was an understatement describing our loss. Lois chose a Tamoxifin regimen for the next five years as a follow-up cancer treatment from the list of options her doctor recommended.

After everything that happened, I knew I needed to escape, to turn my back on everything, get this great loss behind me by sailing on the high seas of our world. All of our dear friends and family tried to assist us in getting away. Our bridge club even presented us with a ship's bell to connect us with Eddie, and to celebrate his life as we traveled. I tried to ring it every day, and in doing so we both felt Eddie's presence aboard.

After making arrangements concerning the management of our business and selling our house, finally in the fall of 1997 we left

Sandusky with our family aboard, and headed off on this momentous voyage. We only traveled 25 miles to the first port, but nevertheless we were underway. We stopped in Lorain for one last farewell party and said goodbye to our children and grandchildren.

We sailed northeast on Lake Erie to the Welland Canal into Lake Ontario to Toronto to see the "Phantom of the Opera" one last time. From Toronto we sailed to Oswego, New York, and onto the Erie Barge Canal. The grand canal gently got us to the head of the Hudson River at Albany. Two days on the Hudson River past theTwin Towers and the Statue of Liberty, we found a protected haven in Great Kills Harbor on Staten Island.

Sailing down the Hudson we both kept saying we shouldn't be here without Ed. He should be with us. We had spent hours and hours delivering boats with Eddie traveling this same route. In 1980 Lois and I had attended the Annapolis Boat Show, and independently spotted the boat we both loved. We couldn't afford to buy it so we came up with an alternative plan—we would become the dealers for the Great Lakes region. We hopped a plane to Florida and talked to Jim Krogen, a well-known naval architect, and made our offer. He was delighted to expand to the Great Lakes, and eventually Eddie came back home to work in our auxiliary business of semi-custom yacht sales.

"We had so much fun working and traveling to the various boat shows with Ed. He was so likeable he could sell anything to anyone," Lois often says.

Eddie and I were more than a father and a son during all those yacht delivery trips on the Hudson. We were great friends who shared like interests—boats.

At his funeral at Grace United Methodist Church in Vermilion, we heard many stories of what Eddie meant in other people's lives. Lois recalls, "As president of the senior class at Vermilion High School, it was his job to man the pop stands at the Woolly Bear Festival. He intentionally asked all the kids who never got to do anything, and got them involved working the stands. That was the kind of person he was. When he gave his speech as president he said, 'I love every single one of you.'"

Lois smiles as she remembers "Trish, the Dish," as Ed called her, showing up at our front door prior to his funeral with 48 rolls of toilet paper. She said she had just driven here from Florida to attend Eddie's service. En route she tried to think what we might need with all of Eddie's friends coming to our house, thus the toilet paper.

Many young adults who had known or worked with him at Friday's Restaurant came to Eddie's service from New York and New Jersey.

Later those same youngsters saved their tips from a whole weekend and asked Lois and me if we would use that money to start a scholarship fund in Eddie's honor. We thought it a great idea, and quickly set up a memorial scholarship at Vermilion High School. Every year we get to select the recipient for the Ed Babson Scholarship Award from the dozens of essays that are submitted by the students applying. Eddie keeps on giving even when gone.

Mementos celebrating Eddie's life are still placed by his grave site by his friends. We go there occasionally, and are grateful to find them.

Lois tells how Ed played a part in bringing *Que Sera Sera* into our lives: "We had bought two Krogen's for personal use in six years, sold them both, and were expecting our third one. I called Jim Krogen and asked when it was going to be shipped, expecting to live aboard our boat on weekends. When Jim told me that the new boat had not been built yet, I told him that we have eight phone lines coming into our home on weekends, when our fluid power business is closed and when spring comes, we move onto the boat so we don't have to listen to the phone. Cancel the order."

Because Eddie had picked up another line, Hans Christian, we were willing to try whatever was available. When we flew to Mexico to charter a Hans Christian, we were disappointed. She rolled and was very hard to maneuver. But when our boat arrived it was the Christina 40 contemporary model, and not the model we had tested. After putting it in the boat show three years in a row, it was time for us to buy her!

We named her *Que Sera Sera*—whatever will be will be. She is the perfect ocean-going boat. We would never sail anything else. Over time *Que Sera Sera* has come to summarize our attitude toward life.

Lois and I sailed down the east coast to the Chesapeake Bay, and sampled its great fresh seafood. We paused two weeks in Annapolis, spending many days with Ralph Nehrig and Ann Harsh from Cleveland, Ohio. They had joined the rally on the yacht, *Harmonie*. We proceeded further south through the tidewaters of the Carolinas and Georgia to Florida. Friends found us a protected haven at Grand Harbor in Vero Beach, and we holed up for the winter under the warm Florida sun.

Lois and I often felt Eddie's presence as we worked through our pain and grief. Lois recalls a windy day on a Ft. Lauderdale beach when crews were using snowplows to get the blowing sand off the road nearby. "As I was walking the beach, two balloons blew off the ocean toward me and wrapped around my feet. They were from a Friday's which is where Eddie used to work."

In May we moved the boat north to St. Augustine, Florida, where we joined the Trans Arc Rally to Europe. Our son Fred and his wife

Shelly were aboard for this first offshore leg to Bermuda to lend a hand. It was a good thing they were because the autopilot died four days out of port and we had to hand steer day and night for three days. After being overcome by a huge frontal system storm with winds of 50 plus knots, we arrived in Bermuda, now knowing that both Lois and I and our sturdy craft could safely complete the voyage.

Lois and I sailed the long 14-day-leg from Bermuda to the Azores across the open North Atlantic Ocean on our own. We spent two weeks sightseeing those wonderful islands in the Azores before continuing on to Ireland, where we spent two and half months sailing the Celtic Sea and the English Channel to London. *Que Sera Sera* handled well on our long crossings even when the winds continued to blow from 28 to 35 knots day after day. In these conditions, we sailed very fast, making as many as 178 miles in a 24-hour period.

The seas were huge. We had to hang on or be thrown around. There is an old saying that certainly applied then, "One hand for the ship and one for yourself." The galley "slave" had to be sure she was strapped to the safety bar when she needed two hands to prepare our meals. Often the huge waves would rise high above the stern of our now, very small boat and tumble forward as they raced along past us. Fifteen-foot waves would not actually fall in the cockpit, but rather push us forward rapidly as the waves surged under the boat, propelling our 12-ton boat forward at eight plus knots.

Our day-to-day routine aboard *Que Sera Sera* kept us busy during our Atlantic crossing. Life was pretty easy while at sea and by the third day we got into a very comfortable routine. Lois is a morning person and at home is often up by five, so I did the night watch from 8 to 2:30 or 3. Because we had the autohelm, we felt six-hour watches gave us both a full night of sleep. Night watches were usually pleasant and peaceful under a clear, star- filled sky. The stars out on the sea were so plentiful, providing enough light and good visibility in all directions. It is easier to see ships much further away than in the daylight.

After a meal similar to what we would have at home, Lois filled a thermos with coffee before she went to bed. I usually had my first cup around midnight with a few cookies to go with it. I needed the caffeine to continue my book reading. We both read with a miner's type head lamp on our heads. I read at night. Lois read around the clock, and quickly joined the book-a-day club.

We also spent time playing Free Cell on our extra computer. It made the hours fly by. In addition we did manual chart plotting regularly even though we use our GPS all the time. Our radar alerted us if anything came within eight miles of us. The person off-watch slept in the aft stateroom so he or she could hear a call for help, if necessary. Lois woke me if we needed to make a serious adjustment in our sails. The night flew by as we studied the constellations, and compared our findings when our mate came on watch.

We are often asked how we were able to spend so much time together. Delightfully, we reply because we had 12 hours a day when we were not together, which was our private and personal time. Lois often would give herself a pedicure, shave her legs, plan meals and spend time meditating when she wasn't reading or working on her photo albums.

Our 27-day journey across the Atlantic allowed Lois and me time for reflection. We realized that we have been lifetime partners for each other. Partners in business, partners in marriage, friendship and now partners in grief.

We actually go way back to junior high school in Willoughby, Ohio. As Lois says,"We were best friends in school. Don helped me learn how to drive. We were in high school band together. Later at Bowling Green people used to ask what is it with you two? You radiate an attraction for each other."

Upon graduation, I was looking for work after college as an industrial arts teacher. Those positions were hard to find in Florida, so I ended up teaching Seminole Indians and Mexicans in Immokalee, Florida. Lois was able to teach fourth grade with her degree in Health and Physical Education.

Our first business venture together was watermelon farming. We were sure our agricultural enterprise would supplement our meager teachers' salaries with a return of at least $10,000. A local farmer loaned us 10 acres to plant. After coaxing the seeds to sprout by soaking them in milk in a bathtub, we planted the whole field by hand, and then covered the plants with tar paper tents at night, taking them off on our way to teach in the morning. After we paid for the seed, our night watchmen and the crop dusters, we didn't make a dime because the truckers had already moved on following the crops north.

Neither of us has been afraid to take risks. Risk taking seems to come naturally somehow. Upon returning to northern Ohio, a response to a newspaper ad led me into a new career in industrial sales. After working four years as a salesman for Eagle Equipment, a fluid power company out of Columbus, Ohio, the opportunity came to take the biggest risk yet—starting our own business.

"On Don's 40th birthday, he calls me and says the distributor that he was working for has changed product lines. We are going to pick up their old lines that they are dropping, and go into business for ourselves," Lois remembers.

Emboldened by this simple declaration, we started Babson Fluid Power, Inc. in 1976 in Huron, Ohio. Our fluid power company supplies hydraulic and pneumatic equipment for industry and businesses—"the muscles of automation."

"I took out every book in the library about how to start a business. We didn't have a nickel to our names and no insurance, but it was an exciting thing to do," she says.

"So we were operating out of our bedroom with cardboard boxes and a Smith Corona typewriter. When the phone would ring, I would say I will let one of our salesman know you called, as if we had several."

Lois says "The physical education teacher was sure *she* had the answers and the industrial arts teacher thought that *he* knew it all." That's when we went to Marriage Encounter, and learned to work together by having better communication.

In the fall of 1996, Lois and I were faced with the most monumental challenge our marriage would ever encounter. How would we cope with the impending trial of the woman who had killed our son? Grappling with that decision caused our whole family to search the depths of our souls for answers.

Lois recalls, "We were at home sitting around our kitchen table with Dee and Fred, and their spouses, Kevin and Shelly, trying to figure out how something good could come out of this disaster. We asked ourselves what would Eddie do? He would be furious, but after he got that out of his system, he also would have been understanding. He would be the first to forgive."

We made the decision to fly back to Nassau County, New York to attend the trial. Lois and I had decided to ask the judge to rule in favor of community service, rather than prison for Deana Yakkey. We had lost our son, and now Deana was going to lose her life in jail. We asked ourselves if we could do something better, if we could make some good come out of bad. I believe it was because of this lifetime partnership and our faith that we were able to make this difficult decision together.

One of our dear friends, Rhonda Watt, a guidance counselor in Port Clinton, had suggested that Deana tell this tragic story to students to encourage them to take responsibility for their actions regarding drinking and driving. The prosecuting attorney in Nassau County was very reluctant to entertain our suggestion, but after interviewing Deana, they felt that she was truly remorseful, and saw that she had no previous record, so they agreed to let her proceed.

When we spoke to the judge personally, he said he had never seen anything like this in his 26 years on the bench. He had always sentenced drunk drivers who killed someone to a jail sentence.

After reviewing the powerful impact Deana's story had on students, he recommended five years' probation. "I don't think retribution is as important as what the Babsons asked me to do," he said. "She is doing more penitence having to retell this tragic story for five years than if she were put in jail."

Later, this same judge was visibly moved as he appeared with Lois and me on "The Today Show" and on MSNBC News in June 1997, and recounted his decision to honor our request for community service. His very generous comment was "They are superior human beings, and I could not deny them what they wanted."

We had sent Deana three life-size photo posters of Eddie so that she could show them to her audiences, and they would know our son and his zest for life. We enclosed a letter to her saying, "Best of luck! We know it will be hard but might help save others this awful pain."

Deana was shocked when the judge ordered community service. She was prepared to go to prison knowing that this judge had always given drunk drivers extensive jail time.

Eddie was at the top of the mountain in his young life when he was killed. We told Deana she needed to carry his light. In the courthouse she responded by saying, "I need to carry his light for you." And she did so faithfully during those five years.

After the trial I slowly began to let go of my anger. I realized that when you are full of hate and think about it often, it just grinds in your gut.

Lois describes her experience of letting go of anger and intense grief this way: "I believe it was Eddie's time to die. I would rather he go this way than suffer from a long illness. I think of him as being with us often. How do we know that heaven isn't here, but on a different plane like when a propeller on a airplane goes around? You can't see it, but it is actually there."

Our reminiscing ended as the vast ocean lay behind us and we harbor-hopped along the southern coast of Ireland, Wales, and England. As Lois said, "We aren't on vacation. We are actually living in foreign countries mixing with the locals as we shop, do our laundry, and tour."

We often thought about Eddie as we sailed away from reality. But now with clearer minds, we welcome the many memories of our good times together with him. The ocean wind and waves have helped carry away our tears.

The *Millennium Odyssey Rally*

The Milleniu

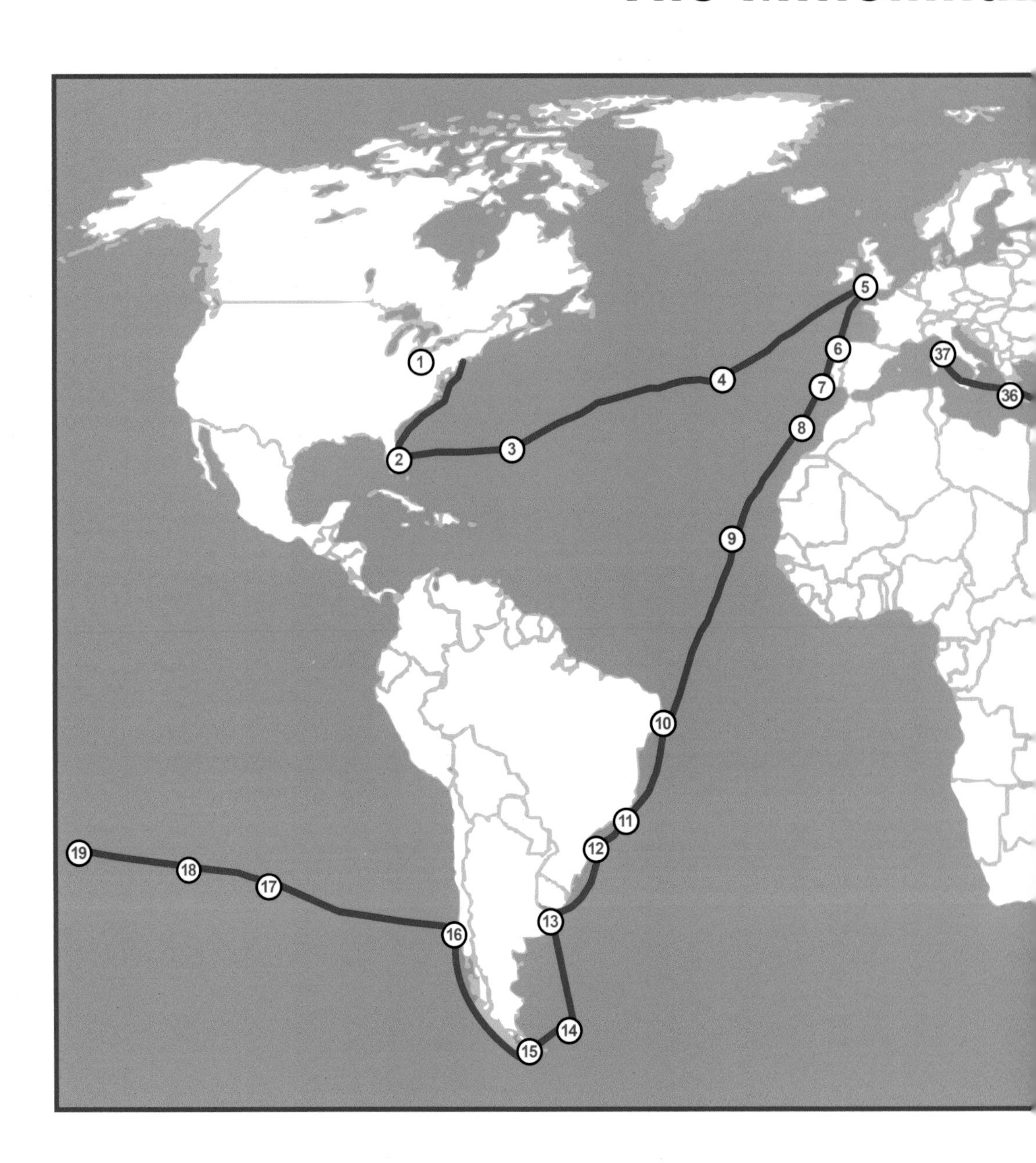

1. Sandusky 2. St. Augustine, Fla. 3. Bermuda 4. Azores 5. Ireland & England - The Rally Begins 6. La Coruna, Spain	7. Lisbon, Portugal 8. Canary Islands 9. Cape Verde Islands 10. Recife, Brazil 11. Salvador, Brazil 12. Rio De Janeiro, Brazil 13. Mar Del Plata, Argentina	14. Falkland Islands 15. Puerto Williams, Ch 16. Valdivia, Chile 17. Easter Island 18. Pitcairn Island 19. Tuamotu Islands 20. Papeete, Tahiti

Odyssey Rally

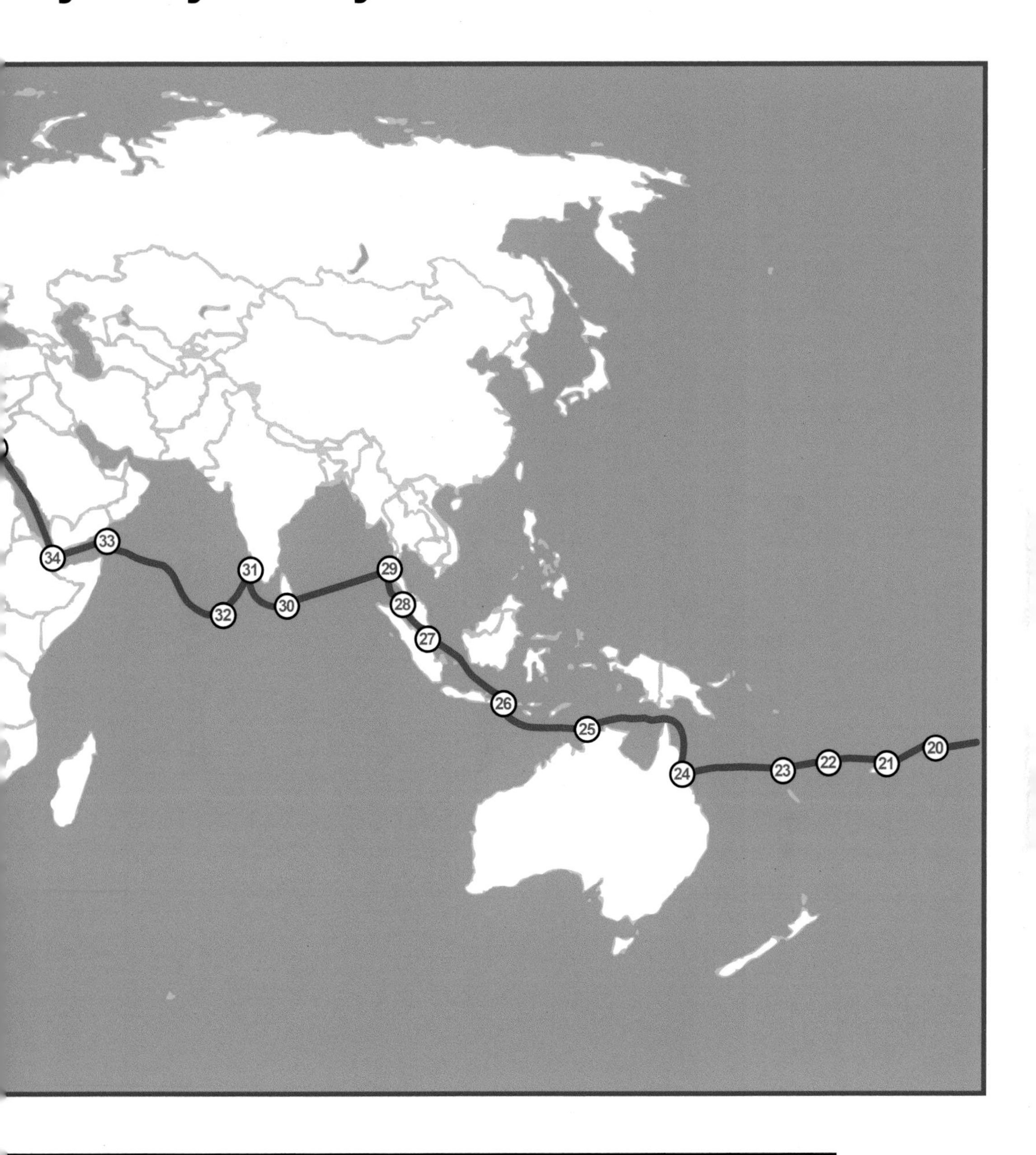

1. Kingdom of Tonga	28. Malaysia	35. Port Suez, Egypt
2. Fiji	29. Phuket, Thailand	36. Crete, Greece
3. Vanuatu Islands	30. Sri Lanka	37. Rome, Italy - The Rally Ends
4. Cairns, Australia	31. Cochin, India	
5. Darwin	32. Maldives Islands	
6. Bali	33. Malacca, Yemen	
7. Singapore	34. Djibouti	

Que Sera Sera at the starting line of the Millennium Odyssey Rally under the Tower Bridge in London

2

The Millennium Rally Begins

Editor's Note:

The following pages were excerpted from the journals of Don and Lois

Que Sera Sera and six other yachts in our fleet are lowered down 28 feet by locks to the Thames River, in the shadow of the Tower of London, on September 12, 1998. Lois and I are filled with excitement awaiting the start of the two-year Millennium Rally we have so long anticipated.

We are caught up in the historical significance of being part of the first ever round-the-world yacht race to visit all six continents. The lanterns aboard each of our boats carry a flame which was lit at the Church of the Holy Sepulchre in Jerusalem and will be transported to 40 different cultures during moving flame ceremonies.

Jimmy Cornell, president of the World Cruising Club, and organizer of the Millennium Rally, is present at our start in London as he actually will travel as part of the fleet on *Adventura III*. Jimmy was raised in Romania under a repressive communist rule and had seen his own father choose death rather than falsely state that he was loyal to the regime. It is his vision that brought us all here. In his book *Jimmy Cornell, A Passion for the Sea, Reflections of Three Circumnavigations*, Jimmy writes, "This would be an opportunity not only to celebrate the arrival of a new millennium, but much more important, to mark a milestone in the history of mankind, that after the fall of communism, promised to usher in an age of peace, international harmony and understanding."

Cornell continues, "Looking back into the early history of man, I saw that the gift of fire to another clan or tribe must have been the original symbol of peace, an early instance of man stretching out his hand in help to a fellow human being. My idea therefore was for a symbolic Millennium Flame to circle the globe and bring everywhere a message of hope, understanding and, above all, peace."

Now locked down to the Thames River from St. Katherine's Dock, we are led by a police patrol boat a few hundred yards under the historic Tower Bridge. It has been raised for our passage into an area between the Tower Bridge and the new London Bridge, five city blocks further up river. Here we mill around in the out-flowing tide while waiting for the second half of the rally fleet to be locked down to join us.

After a half an hour, we get word from our escort vessel that the rest of the fleet is now trapped in St. Katherine's dock. A small bridge that must be opened to enter the lock has failed to open. So they will not be able to join with us in time for the start.

With that news, all haste is made by our small fleet to make sail and head for the starting line—the Tower Bridge. It has once again been raised for us much to the distress of the car traffic waiting to cross. I might add that the Tower Bridge is a main traffic bridge of four lanes in downtown London so is seldom raised except for special occasions. We proceed under the historic bridge with our big white, yellow and black spinnaker set and flying.

Amid horns blaring, cannon blasting, press helicopters chop-chopping overhead and chase boats following along, we wave to all and sail our way down river toward the English Channel 28 miles away. We pass Greenwich on the International Dateline from which all time is started and the historic marine museum where Sir Frances Chichester's famed yacht *Gypsy Moth* is on display. Then, with the tide flowing with us, we slip through the famous Thames River tide barrier gates that cross the breadth of this big waterway. Our four-hour trip down the historic river is fast, fun and euphoric.

Little did we realize what awaited us at the Thames delta and the English Channel on our leg to the Isle of Wight. In a word BAD—bad head winds, bad sharp seas on the bow, bad for the tide turned heavy against us, bad night of shipping traffic as we beat slowly past the Cliffs of Dover. Off to port bad shallow shoal areas run along parallel to the shore marked with red and green navigation lights blinking all around.

We bash westward all night and the next day as well, finally arriving in the dark of the night at Cowes on the Isle Of Wright. Here it was that we nearly collide with our good friends Ralph and Ann, on *Harmonie* as they quickly and unexpectedly emerge from amidst the many moored yachts swinging in the anchorage. The depressing thing was that Ralph and Ann had started from London several hours later than we had due to the problems with the lock at St. Katherine's Dock. Now, here they are almost running us over in the dark of night.

This is by far the longest bashing to windward since we departed Ohio almost a year before. We are lucky to have sailing friends, Bill and Marlene Noyes, from Huron, Ohio aboard to help stand watch during this slog, for it would have been totally miserable to have tried it with just the two of us.

After three days of recuperation and some parties at the Cowes

Sailing and Rowing Club sponsored by the rally organizers, we are ready to head off again.

When we get out to the Solent, the winds are still strong from the west and so we did some more bashing to windward for several hours. It is so choppy we back the headsail and heave to for lunch. After the hour-long break, the wind goes more northerly, and we have gotten far enough west to be able to head southwest as well. Beam reaching in 20 knots is not so bad and now we are making good speed toward the northwest corner of France.

The first night, all is fine aboard *Que Sera Sera*, with the crew each taking two-hour watches with plenty of shipping to keep us awake. The next day is dawning beautifully under clear blue skies with a broad reach, and we are making seven plus knots across the Bay of Biscay toward Spain.

Then disaster strikes. Marlene tips the gimbaled stove in the galley dumping the entire contents of the freshly brewed coffee pot onto her left shoulder. By accident she grabbed the movable stove to steady herself as she tried to stand after cleaning something off the floor below the stove. The coffee is scalding hot and instantly soaks into the polar fleece sweater she is wearing, which starts to cook the skin off her arm.

She reacts quickly, and with a shout for help she yanks the sweater over her head only to burn her ear as well. All of us were staring at the raw flesh exposed on her entire arm and neck wondering what should we do now.

Although we were sailing at close to seven knots, we start the engine to add a half a knot to get her to a doctor and call for help. We text message rally control in London on our Immersat communication system. We also contact *Harmonie* on the same system, for they are the closest to us. This is Sunday, but we hear back from rally control within a half an hour and *Harmonie* even sooner. Ann on *Harmonie* looks in her burn book and advises us to wrap the burn in galley plastic wrap and treat her for shock. We wrap her arm as instructed but luckily Marlene shows no symptoms of shock. Some of the rest of us may be in shock but Marlene seems fine.

Cape Finisterre Coast Guard calls us on our radio and asks if we need immediate assistance. They could send a helicopter to us within two hours if necessary, but the way the seas are running, we are an unsteady target for a helicopter. We decline their offer.

Rally control advises us that the nearest port is La Coruna, Spain, about 12 hours on a slightly more easterly course than our present course to Porto, Portugal, our first stop on this leg, so we change course and make all speed for La Coruna.

When in a hurry to get off the water, the light seems to fade extra fast. Just try to find the harbor entry lights of a strange new port in the dark of the night. We find the extra-dim pier head light and turn hard to starboard behind the wall where we see a myriad of small white lights, and a lot of sailboat spars stretching upward into the dark heaven above the water. Where there are masts there is a marina. At creep speed we head toward the beckoning masts, and find an empty dock waiting that had been reserved for us. We arrive just short of midnight. The marina watchman calls a cab for Marlene and Bill to take them to the hospital.

After a short night in a strange, unanticipated port, we wake up to discover La Coruna—a big city surrounding us on three sides. Arriving in the dark, we could not even get a hint of what was to appear with the morning light. The old Spanish city is large and historic with a backdrop of new modern buildings located in the encircling hills.

Bill returns to *Que Sera Sera at* about 11 in the morning just a little worse for wear. He had checked Marlene into a very modern hospital that has a special burn unit and then slept in the lobby until morning. Finding her doing well and in good spirits, he came back to the boat to apprise us of her condition. We walk up into the old city area, have lunch, and debate how we should proceed onto Porto, our original destination. The doctors demand that Marlene be confined to her bed for at least seven days and maybe longer. Lois and I stay aboard that night, but Bill goes back to the hospital to stay with Marlene.

Lois and I catch a cab to the hospital early the next morning to see Marlene and Bill. Marlene is doing just fine and is in good spirits again. We take some photos of the three of us with our patient and then begin discussing how to get to Porto. We decide that Lois and I would leave early the next morning, and try to catch up with the fleet there. Knowing that Marlene would not be allowed back on the boat for two weeks, we make arrangements to meet in Lisbon, Portugal. They gladly agree to this alternative plan, but it was certainly hard for all of us to be parting with one of our crew still in the hospital.

Sadly Bill and Marlene never did join us because the doctors would not allow her to travel in case she might accidentally bump or scrape her skinless arm. After two weeks in the hospital, they got on an airplane and flew back to Ohio; their trip ended 30 days earlier than planned.

An interesting aside to the hospital stay was that the Spanish socialistic government paid for the entire hospital stay and all the doctors' fees as well. Bill tried to pay them, but they had no means to bill or charge a private person for medical work.

Underway again, we still find some sailing winds to head west and we round one of the great capes, Cape Finisterre, just after midnight.

Sailing past big land masses like a cape or a high hill seems to take forever, for they are so large, and we go so slowly. The lighthouse high on the tip of the cape appears just before sunset, but because we must first sail past the north side of it and then turn due south, it is still abeam as the eight bells of midnight ring.

To put the famous cape finally behind us was a memorable milestone in our journey. On arriving in Porto, Portugal, we find the fleet crews scattered all about the big city doing some shopping, sightseeing, and hearty eating ashore. Ann and Ralph return to the docks in the mid-afternoon to welcome us and invite us for dinner aboard *Harmonie.* The rally had arranged for all of the fleet to be hosted by a sherry wine Bodegas. A good time was had by all as we sip very old sherry, eat hors d'oeuvres and tour the wine-making museum. We are starting now to appreciate what a good thing it was to join the rally, for we sure have had some fine parties and special events sponsored by the rally, and at no additional cost to us.

I'd like to review the rules of the rally. First being a rally, we have a start and a finish on each leg of the event. Then at special cocktail parties at the new port, awards are presented to the first, second and third place winners of the race. All boats have a handicap according to their size. We, being the smallest, have a very large handicap when we are racing boats as large as a 90-foot Swan to Jimmy Cornell's Onvi 43, the closest to our size.

A rally participant is allowed to use his or her engine to advance toward the finish. If one does use the engine, however, he will be penalized an extra hour and a half for each hour in use. Therefore, you must record exactly when the engine comes on and when it is turned off. For us it was of no use to turn on the engine if we were doing more than four knots for we can only motor at six knots.

Something the captain must consider is that, if the winds are really light and he doesn't turn on the engine, he might miss the welcoming party at the finish. He may have a mutiny on his hands if his crew misses out on all the good food, drink and conversation.

The leg prizes are usually pretty clever. Over the course of the two years we did get three third places. Our big handicap really helps.

We find one of the drawbacks is barging at the fuel dock. Recall that we had run our engine all day across the Bay of Biscay trying to get Marlene to the hospital and for a day and a half getting to Porto. Also remember that the whole fleet had been in the port for at least four days before we arrived. The evening before we were to depart, I made an appointment to get fuel at the gas dock at 8:30 a.m. We cast off our lines and motor over to the gas dock, and find two of our rally yachts already tied up there waiting for the dock to open. As there was no room for us on the dock, we turned around and motored to a larger area in the harbor to wait patiently for them to get their fuel and leave.

We will no longer make the ten o'clock start outside the break wall. Due to these delays, we were the last boat to cross the starting line, but it was a good sailing day and we were at sea once again. Lisbon, here we come.

This leg to Lisbon is a light air leg and our heavy, short water line craft does not do so well, but we keep sailing slowly south trying to get maybe a third or even a fourth place finish.

The last night before reaching Lisbon, the winds die altogether and on comes Denny, the diesel engine. This is good for the seas calm and the ever-steady droning of the motor hums the off-watch into a sound sleep and we should get there in time for the welcome party.

The next day we are still motoring along on an unusual calm ocean when we overtake *Adventura 111*, Jimmy Cornell's go-fast centerboard cutter. It is easy because we are motoring and he is sailing. He is chasing a small zephyr from the nearby land to our east. Unfortunately for him the zephyr is taking him out to sea to the west and not south to Lisbon.

I call Jimmy on our radio, and inquire about his choice of a sailing direction. I try to be very polite and not suggest to him that his course is a poor one. Eventually Jimmy confesses that his perfect, new boat has a fuel problem and that he cannot motor. After more discussion, we agree that *Que Sera Sera* will take *Adventura 111* in tow.

We rig a towing bridle on our stern and attach a 200-foot long towline and take him in tow. One of the great things about a light weight, go-fast boat is that when we take him in tow, we could still maintain our normal cruising speed of five and a half knots over the bottom.

Once in the Tagus River, we pass the imposing large statue of Henry the Navigator to port and the massive hilltop statue of Jesus to starboard. We make it past the huge shipyards on the bend in the river and almost to the entry to the docks of the Expo 98, which is where we are to dock.

We make it to Lisbon before dark, but not to the dock before we are run over by a squall. We are only 20 minutes away from safety when the winds strike. Jimmy, seeing the darkening clouds, calls ahead to his staff waiting for us at the expo. They find us an almost empty marina just five minutes away and we proceed rapidly to it as the winds continue to build. We get Jimmy's boat near a dock and he casts off our towline. Luckily Jimmy's staff are here to take our lines, for now the winds are howling strongly and the black clouds are dropping their water in heavy sheets. We are here, Lisbon!

3

Lisbon to the Canary Islands

Expo 98 was to end the day our rally fleet left Lisbon; therefore our rally organizers were able to get our entire fleet free dockage inside the main marine display dock area where we could moor next to some old sailing relics. Nearby was a frigate, the second-largest square rigger in the world from Argentina and the fifth-largest square rigger from Spain.

As the expo ends, we are among the first boats to depart from the many vessels assembled there. Our starting line is only a few hundred yards off the spectator-covered shore. We do some probing for a good place on the starting line, and seem ready to plunge across the line when our headsail gets wrapped around the forestay. The only way to free it is for me to go forward, and pull it manually across the deck.

I get that done, but in the process the fast flowing river turns the boat back on the other tack. As I return to the helm, we need to re-tack the sail. As it gets wrapped around again, we sail away farther from the starting line rather than across it. The captain issues a few curse words, noticing all of the hundreds of spectators on shore. Once we were first, now we are last.

We do finally get ourselves straightened out, and we sail an hour south down the Tagus River where we drop sail and pull into a gas dock to top off our fuel.

Full of fuel we once again set sail out to the Atlantic where black clouds and bolts of lighting streaking across the sky await us. It looks to be a bad night to head out, but it must be going the same way we are, only faster, for we never had to endure any adverse effects from the dark storm.

After two easy sailing days and nights and one 24-hour-bash to windward day and night, we arrive in Madeira with a guest aboard. The second day at sea we had a small bird fly aboard. At the time the weather was good, but the bird must have known that an ill wind was brewing for that night the winds picked up from forward of the beam. The spray got so bad that our little feathered friend went below and hid on a shelf in the main salon. It didn't reappear until the winds calmed in mid-morning.

Finally it flies out from below, lands on the binnacle, less than three feet from us, seems to gaze directly at us for a couple of minutes as if to say thanks and then flies off towards Madeira, which was now clearly in sight.

Sometimes the last boat in has some advantages. Instead of having to tie up to a high, slimy wall, we get to tie up to another rally yacht away from the wall. We are the fifth boat out. Climbing over four boats to get to the rope ladder to climb up the wall is not easy, but is much better than having our little ship bashing against the wall.

We spend several days touring this lush mountainous island and getting to know other participants of the rally fleet. We revisit the special ship restaurant which was a square-rigged sailing vessel of old, placed high and dry on the shore by one of the Beatles, Ringo Star, methinks.

We get to know a young couple from Germany, Ralf and Inge, who are sailing a Caribbean 40 which Ralf had built himself. We thought they would be our closest racing competitor.

Within an hour after we clear the high mountain's wind shadow, we begin to experience higher winds. All sails are set once again and off we go. Nice sailing for one hour, but then comes the normal trade winds of 20-plus and all of us are over canvassed.

We put a reef in the main. One reef reduces our sail by about 30 percent and we furl, wrap up our headsail all together, and blast on with the staysail set on an easy beat to windward. This happens, of course, as night is descending upon us. After seven days in a calm safe harbor we are now out on some big, lumpy ocean waves getting knocked all over the place in the dark of the night.

We are doing sort of OK until 10 p.m. when we feel a violent shaking going on aboard. "What's that?" the mate asks the skipper. "Gee, I don't know," answers the skipper. "Well, find out," the mate gently requests of the skipper. "OK, honey," answers the skipper as he dons his life jacket and harness and heads forward on the bouncing deck. "Well, GOSH DARN IT," exclaims the skipper as he sights the headsail starting to unfurl off the headstay. "Don't worry, honey, I'll get it." Perhaps there is more to this story, but let's just say we got safely through the night.

With the light of the morning brightening our attitude, we sight our new friends, Ralf and Inge, just a half a mile to our port side so we call them on the VHS radio. The response is not good. The mate is very somber and she relates how her skipper had been nearly choked to death by the main sheet. As he jibed the boat, the mainsail swung from one side of the boat to the other. In the process, the main sheet lines, which are connected to the floor of the cockpit, caught around his neck and flung him across to the opposite side of the cockpit. He fetched up tight on the other tack with the lines virtually strangling him. He struggled free after a few minutes, but he was very bruised and feeling sick.

After a short sail of 280 nautical miles, we arrive in the new marina at Pureto Calero on the island of Lanzarote. Here we find a fine large modern marina with floating side tie docks for about 200 boats.

Upon our arrival, the docks are full of either permanent dock holders or the many voyagers getting ready to cross the Atlantic to the Caribbean for the winter. So we get to tie to another high concrete wall.

Here in Puerto Calero, we also received our brass lamp of hope, peace, and goodwill from one of the boats that had started in Jerusalem during a ceremony presided over by our rally organizer, Jimmy Cornell. It was a very exciting and memorable occasion because the lamp had been lit at Jesus' tomb in the Church of the Holy Sepulchre.

The lighting of the lamps in the tomb was the first time a Roman Catholic and a Greek Orthodox priest joined together in performing a ceremony. Our lamps were already bringing peace.

We would be passing the flame on every continent to which we sailed. Our lamp was lit by a young Italian couple, Alfredo and Nicoletta, who are sailing a 52 foot Mikados. They had participated in the original ceremony in Israel.

Our job was to keep our lamp lit on our boat so we could pass on the flame. When we attended our first flame-passing here in Lanzarote, an official from the island signed our log book as would happen each time we stopped to pass on the flame around the world.

After an emotional celebration, we return to *Que Sera*, and proceed to drill two holes in the main salon forward bulkhead and bolt our bright, brass gimbaled lantern safely out of harm's way. Even safely secured, it is clearly visible to all who board the boat.

The lamp did require some attention because I had to refill the lamp reservoir every seven to eight days with kerosene. The other important time-consuming job was to keep it shining brightly. This took some effort because salt-water-saturated air soon turns bright brass dull, then dark. The skipper of *Vegawind* caught the wrath of Jimmy Cornell in Recife, Brazil, when he carried a very blackened lamp.

After four days of rest and replenishment, the remainder of the fleet left to do the Round the Canary's race. We did not join this race, but rather chose to recover and relax in the warm and sunny atmosphere of the island. We felt rather responsible for our strangled friend, so we stayed behind with Ralf and his wife, Inge. He was slow to recover from his near disaster and was in no shape to do another grueling race.

We hang around for a week, being tourists as we rode camels, hiked the subterranean volcanic grottoes, and the cactus gardens while touring with Ralf and Inge. Lanzarote is an enchanting island where the astronauts trained before they went to the moon and where the movie "Planet of the Apes" was filmed. This island is covered with either sand from the Sahara Desert or volcanic ash, depending on the location.

By the way, our Millennium Odyssey Rally was sponsored by the government of the Canary Islands to promote the unique attractions on this archipelago.

We sail south along the eastern coast of Lanzarote by ourselves for our German friends were still not ready to set off.

When we get to the south end of the island, we decide not to sail all the way to the next island west, Fortaventura, but rather to anchor in a small bay for the rest of the afternoon and to ride the hook there for the evening.

We didn't realize it at the time, but we were anchoring off a nude-bathing beach. In the late afternoon we begin to see people standing up all along the beach gathering their beach gear and putting on their beach wear. Yikes! They were all nude and old. Old, like 75. Old and nude is not a very scenic combination. Let's just say saggy bottoms and droopy bosoms hanging on tired old bodies is an eye closer.

After a stop for an overnight on the island of Fuerteventura, which is the European's Florida, we sail on to Las Palmas on the island of Gran Canaria and join the rest of the fleet, which has now grown to 36 yachts.This is a modern city even though it was established well before Columbus came here on his first trip of discovery. It's a very fine place for re-provisioning our vessels for the impending voyage to the New World.

At the marina we have *Que Sera Sera* hauled out to clean the bottom and propeller. After all, we have to keep up with some big, fast yachts on the legs to Chile.

We will be leaving the main fleet of the rally, for the rest are heading for the Caribbean while we head south to Brazil. Our fleet of seven yachts includes the following: *Vegawind,* a steel 60′ schooner; *Futuro,* a 65′ Swan from Germany; *Happy Spirit,* an Ocean 60 from Britain; *Risqué,* a 57′ Swan from Wisconsin; *Harmonie,* a 53′ Amel from Cleveland, Ohio, and Jimmy Cornell's 43′ aluminum go-fast centerboard sloop from France. A mid-morning start sees *Que Sera Sera* positioned second over the starting line, just scant feet behind *Risqué,* not bad for *Risqué* has an experienced racing crew of six aboard. Just being the two of us, things tend to go a little slower aboard than that crack bunch of aggressive sailors. With that nice start we head off once more on another open ocean crossing of 810 nautical miles to the Cape Verde Islands.

4

Cape Verde Islands To Brazil

By sunrise there are no other yachts of our fleet of seven to be seen. The wind is very light and we hoist our asymmetrical spinnaker and later our drifter reacher as well We are colorful to be sure for the big spinnaker is white, black and yellow, and the drifter is red, green, blue, orange and yellow.

The second day as we sail slowly along at three knots, the big blue German yacht, *Vegawind,* comes motoring along and past us about a mile off our beam. They no more than get in front of us when they stop the engine and start hoisting sails. Several sails for she is a two masted 60′ schooner.

They sail along with us for the afternoon, but by sunset are hull down over the horizon. Little did we know at the time, but this brief encounter would lead to the development of a close friendship with one of the crew, Sandra, a vivacious blue-eyed sprite from Scotland.

As we sail in toward the harbor of Mindelo on the island of Sao Vincente, we see the imposing lighthouse standing atop a tall rock island. One could sail on either side of it. According to the charts, the water surrounding it is deep enough that a sailor could literally sail a big ship directly into the side of the rock without hitting bottom.

The harbor here can handle several large container ships, but we are guided further into the harbor by rally control to a smaller commercial dock where we raft off on the outside of two of our fleets' bigger boats. It is a good thing because the dock is so tall and our little *Que Sera Sera* is so small that we could not have gotten off the boat without a ladder.

The Cape Verdes are tall mountainous islands with only marginal natural growth. The large city of Mindelo is new and semi-prosperous, but surrounding the city are small, little huts and decrepit villages that look as though they are barely resisting the ever-present winds.

Two distinct populations live here. The Portuguese, who are the ruling class, were the first to discover and settle here. The African people, who are the working class, were brought here by the Portuguese slave ships. The Portuguese run the businesses and hotels and have money, and the Africans do little and have no money.

This is our first real experience with beggars working the streets. One afternoon after running to the store for paper napkins, Lois was approached by two young boys who asked her for a gift. She told them she had nothing but these paper napkins.

One of the boys asked her for her shirt. "My shirt?" she quickly responded. "Yes, your shirt" "No!" was her instant reply. She wouldn't be caught dead wearing just a bra in public. She was steaming out both ears when she got back aboard *Que Sera Sera.*

Poverty usually leads to thievery and it certainly did here. It was such a problem that before we could dock at the wharf we agreed to pay for a full time around-the-clock watchman. When we depart, we each receive a bill for $300-$400 depending on the length of the yacht.

Water quality seems to be a problem here. Little did we know just how big a problem it would become for us. The first clues were the signs posted around the town stating that water should be boiled for 45 minutes to prevent cholera.

All this aside, we are treated like royalty by the tourist bureau and are guests at two four-star resort hotels' cocktail parties. Nice parties, but at one of them we all got the runs and trots big time the day we left. It was so bad that one yacht with seven people aboard had to return to port for they had no one well enough to stand watches. Nor did they have enough toilets for all of the bottoms that needed to sit all at the same time.

We have one of our worst rally starts as we leave. We didn't beat anyone over the line. I think the reason was that my mate, Lois, was already sick and quite indisposed at the time. A pretty good excuse.

Then southwest onto Brazil only a few days to the southwest, but first we experience another milestone in our trip—crossing the Equator. Eight days and nine nights out of Cape Verde at 0230 hours on a calm sea, we cross the magical line, the equator. This is our first-ever crossing, and we are doing it on our own little sailboat. Wow!

First King Neptune appears in full beard (a shredded plastic bag) properly adorned in a royal robe (a lady's silk house coat). He is sporting a proper crown (cardboard wrapped with shiny aluminum foil) and a trident (fish gaff) in his hand.

King Neptune is soon joined by a beautiful mermaid, sporting a full silver tail (more aluminum foil), and she is showing an almost bare bosom (small bra) and long green hair (a green spinnaker line) adorning her lovely head. What a pair we are way out here on the big ocean in the dark of the night, all alone, but so very happy to be together in this great sailing adventure.

After a few more days of smooth sailing, we happen upon a couple of small, jagged rocky islands sticking up out of the depths of the ocean.

With all credit given to our Micrologic GPS instrument, we are able to find these small specks on this big ocean. As we slowly sail past, we hear someone talking in Portuguese on our VHF radio. An English-speaking male voice comes over the radio calling the sailboat sailing by St. Pedro and St. Paulo Islands. That must be us. No one else is out here.

We are well past the islands by the time he asks us to come over and visit with them, so we decline, but ask him why he is here. His response is that they are part of a six-member Brazilian research team studying hammerhead sharks and dolphins.

We had read that other sailors who had stopped here had encountered many of these huge, fearsome sea creatures. This is one place we would have liked to stop, but as usual we were already three days behind most of the fleet.

As we stand our six-hour watches at night, Lois talks about feeling so close to God and, believing Ed is with God, she is also closer to him. Standing and leaning on our dodger viewing the constellations is always a time to pray and be thankful for all we are experiencing, but also a time to talk to God about the empty hole within us which craves Ed's big hugs. Lois continues to read every book written on life after death, finding answers to her questions which gives her strength. Our "sailing away" is a great help as we slowly come to understand the hold that grief has upon us even as our faith grows stronger.

Seven more days underway sees us approaching a distant shore. A whole new continent—South America. We arrive in the large commercial port of Recife, Brazil shortly after noon, drop anchor and take a two-hour nap. Later we are ready for our rally arrival party that evening at the local Club Naval Yacht Club. It was good to see our fellow travelers again and share our big crossing travails.

At the gathering, we hear a drama recounted. When the first of our rally fleet arrived, they discovered a big, red sailing vessel from Russia. Not long after getting their anchors down, one of the crewmen from the Russian yacht rowed over in a small dinghy and asked Chris, the skipper of *Futuro,* if he had any burn medicine. He said that one of his crew had been burned while at sea four days earlier and that it wasn't healing very well. Chris had some ointment aboard and gave it to the skipper.

The next day as the crew of *Futuro* was taking their dinghy ashore, they stopped by the Russian vessel and asked about the burned sailor.

They reported he was in much pain and they inquired about pain medicine. Chris went back to his boat and got some strong pain killer pills and offered them to the Russian skipper. The skipper then asked if Chris would look at the burned area of his crew member. Chris agreed reluctantly and saw a bad burned lower cheek that was red, inflamed and ugly. The sailor could not sit down and had to lie down on one side of his body.

Apparently the crewman had been changing out of his wet sea pants and, due to an abrupt movement of the boat, backed into the gimbaled stove where a pot of water was boiling. The stove tipped downward and the entire pot of boiling water hit his bare bottom. Did those events ever sound familiar! This sailor required medical attention, but neither he nor anyone on the vessel had enough money to take him to the hospital, let alone pay a hospital bill.

Our rally organizers came to the rescue. The Club Naval offered free medical service at the newly opened health center to any rally participant upon arrival in Recife. Of course the Russian yacht was not a rally participant, but Chris offered to sign the burn victim on as crew for one week. Voila! Free hospitalization. When our fleet left a week later, the Russian was still in the hospital.

From Recife we voyage down the coast of Brazil to Salvador de Bahia, five days south. What a change in scenery! This grand city has transformed itself from an old Portuguese colony into a new thriving city of high-rise buildings, big businesses, big shopping malls and restaurants of the finest quality.

Our arrival in Salvador is a special event. The other rally members are waiting for us on the dock all singing "Que Sera Sera." The marina set off several Roman candle fireworks as we round the harbor wall. Then once docked, we join our friends and the marina manager, who walks down the dock in a white dinner jacket holding a tray with two famous, icy Caipirinha drinks and fresh fruit for us. It was Thanksgiving and we are thankful sailors.

We are very lucky to be here in Salvador for their annual carnival. The word was out that it is second only in size and quality to Rio de Janeiro's.

The rally start is only two days away and that means that we have lots of food shopping and boat stuff to do, but we decide to go to Carnival after completing most of our projects. The rest of our rally friends had gone mid- morning so we would be on our own. No problem for we had previously attended such parades as the Vermilion Woolly Bear parade and the Huron Harbor Fest. Ha! Were we ever naïve! This is a big city by a vast ocean, not a small town on the edge of Lake Erie.

We are warned not to take any valuables and very little money by the dock master. We follow his advice leave our valuables and cash behind, call a cab and off we go to see the parade.

The cabbie drops us off on the top of a small hill in a nice residential area. He tells us the main parade route is just four or five blocks down the hill—that way—as he vaguely points in a northerly direction.

No problem and off we go hand in hand, happy and content in our innocence. As we approach the parade route, we see marching bands and fancy floats. We are totally immersed into the midst of a dark-skinned crowd of people. No one speaks a word of our foreign language. Shouts and much hollering back and forth surround us.

After walking further down the parade route, we find a less crowded place in the ranks of spectators where we can see some of the fantastic floats and the unusually-dressed bands marching by. Then I spot a native man holding a small girl on his shoulders standing next to what looks to be his wife watching the parade. He stands out because he is at least six feet six inches tall and he is smiling a friendly, wide smile to everyone around him. I get quite close to him and hand him my camera. He gives me a blank questioning stare as he looks down to see me tapping his shoulder. I ask him to take some pictures of the tropical-bird costumed people who are passing by. He does not understand so I point at the birds with my camera and then at him again.

That big smile soon floods over us as he takes my camera and starts to snap several pictures. After each of us introduces ourselves to one another, we feel very safe here in this mass of people next to this giant of a man and his family.

The Carnival had started at noon, some miles to the west, and continues until sunset. It is full of color, energy, and music and is a delight to behold. We buy each other beers sold out of ice-filled barrels located in the area. I teach him how to "high five" when a special colorful display passes by. Without ever speaking one word that the other could understand, we communicate perfectly.

The parade is over and we must get back to the marina as it is getting dark. Somehow this man senses our dilemma and leads us back to the main road and hails us a cab. We bid him and his family a fond farewell in English and they all respond likewise in Portuguese and we happily get into the cab. Gesturing to this non-English cab driver where we want to go took a little time. We wonder just where we will end up this night. But we make it home safely. We are ever thankful for our caring new friends, who looked after the innocent Ohioans.

After two fun-filled weeks in Salvador, we sail with the fleet south once more to see the seaside metropolis of Rio de Janeiro. This is not an easy trip for the waters off the coast have hundreds of fishing boats that we must thread our way through day and night. It was especially bad at night, for even with our new radar scanning the way in front of us, we could not see even the largest wooden fishing boats. Radar sees right through wood as if it is not there. Most of them did not have a light, but if they did, it was just one white light hanging over the side of the boat. If the light was hanging over the side we were approaching, we could see it but if it was on the opposite side, of course, we could not. No light. No boat. Well, maybe.

After four nights at sea we make a slight detour to a place on the chart that shows a shallow area of coral reefs that blocks the ever-present ocean swells that keep rocking us from abeam. We arrive at the reef just before midnight and cannot see the location of the entry into the reef, so we slow the boat to a crawl under engine. With only the GPS to guide us, we make our way into a sheltering cove and drop the anchor in 20 feet of very calm water. This is a little nerve wracking, but we are rewarded with a still place to catch up on our sleep.

The next morning upon awakening, we look around for the reef that had protected us, but none was to be seen. Although the chart shows that there is a reef, it really only shows above water on extreme low tides. The rest of the time it is totally under water. We crank up the diesel engine and slowly retrace our GPS inbound path back out into deep water.

In this area we also sail past huge offshore oil rigs. At night we can see the lights on them 20 miles away. Since we are only sailing at four to five knots it seems to take all night to sail past one.

The approach into the large Rio bay is impressive. Everything is so very large. The harbor is long and wide, as big as or even bigger than New York's harbor. There are massive hills behind and on both sides of us as we enter. On the very top of one of the large hills stands a 200-foot statue of Christ with his arms outstretched.

Welcome to the vibrant city of Rio de Janeiro, with its tall buildings and long white sandy beaches of Ipanema and Copacabana. Picture Fort Lauderdale with the mountains of Pennsylvania in the background. The six-mile-long beaches teem with young Brazilians with their bronzed bodies attired in tiny beach wear, either playing volley ball or talking on cell phones at all times of the day.

We are, as usual, the last boat into the small yacht harbor at the Rio Yacht Club so we have lots of help from the crews of the other rally boats. Even so, while backing into the dock, we manage to give the wall a bash. We are happy to see our fellow rally sailors.

Welcome to Rio!

5

Rio to Mar Del Plata

Our good sailing friend, Ken Watt from Huron, Ohio, is scheduled to fly into Rio de Janeiro to sail with us to Argentina. Lois and I rent a car and drive to the airport to meet him.

We soon discover that his duffel bag has been sitting on a baggage cart in the blazing, hot sun during the hour and half it takes to get him cleared through customs and immigration. Once he is cleared, he slings the bag over his shoulder and walks to our waiting rental car. As soon as he throws the bag in the back seat, it becomes apparent that something bad has happened to him for he stinks to high heaven. After questioning him a little bit, we learn the bad odor is not coming from Ken, but rather it is his shirt and duffel bag.

Lois asks him, "Ken what do you have in that bag, three years worth of dirty socks?" "No, a wheel of cheese, Roquefort cheese," he answers.

When we get to the dock at the marina, we dig into the bag and sure enough out comes a 12-inch wheel of strong smelling Roquefort cheese. The wrapping on the cheese had ruptured and the oils had leaked out and into the entire contents of his duffel bag. We wash the cheese wheel at the dock and quickly place it in our refrigerator, but we throw the duffel bag in the trash barrel. Welcome aboard, Ken.

While in Rio, we take in the Ipanema and Copacabana beaches and have lunch at the restaurant where the song "The Girl From Ipanema" was written by a couple of young musicians who were homesick and missed their girlfriends.

We hop on a bus and travel to the top of the mile-high hill behind the city to get a close-up look at the giant statue of Jesus. It is huge, standing over 200 feet tall. The little finger on his hand is six feet long. We are impressed.

On the way to and from the statue, we pass very close to another memorable sight—the slum area. This well-known poverty-stricken area extends from the western city limits up into the hills that surround the thriving city. The area is packed so tightly that no trees or shrubs or even dogs and cats can live. There are no roads, but only small footpaths that exist in the narrow confines of the 50-some square mile area. Poverty is everywhere, leaving people with little hope of ever finding work in the city.

These are mostly rural farming people who never have owned land and have come to the big city by the sea for help. Yet there is no help for them anywhere other than the town dump.

These downtrodden people only have to look up to the top of the next hill to see the statue of the mighty Jesus offering them hope. I pray that as they gaze upward toward those outstretched arms, that it does give them hope. Our rally also is trying to spread the message of hope and goodwill and, although we do not carry our flame of hope into the slums, we carry it to a huge modern Catholic church while in Rio.

The skippers of each of our seven yachts climb aboard a fire truck on our bumpy five-mile ride to the church. Each of us grasp our lighted oil lamps in one hand and hold on for dear life with the other, as we speed down the highway going 50 miles an hour.

First one lamp flame blows out and then another as we accelerate down the road. We are now down to two and now we have none. Smiles turn to concern for we are bringing the flame which had been lit in the Holy Land to the church and now it is gone.

"Don't worry, skippers," our rally agent John Ellis quickly announces, "Don't worry I have brought the Holy Bic," producing a cigarette lighter from his pocket. We try to get our lamps relit, but the howling wind blows them out again. We finally did get them all lit as the fire engine came slowly to a stop in front of the magnificent Catholic church.

This is the largest contemporary-style church that I have ever seen anywhere. We are escorted through a white rose-covered arch into a great courtyard in front of the church and there we join several thousand people who have come in mid-afternoon to witness our flame lighting ceremony. We are greeted warmly by several members of the clergy of the church in their finest robes and colorful religious garments.

After a gathering service held in the courtyard, we make our way into the church sanctuary for the actual flame lighting ceremony. The interior of the church is lit from floor to ceiling by a wall four stories high made of deep blue and purple stained glass. It is indeed an awesome place constructed to serve our awesome God.

We are taught that God is manifest in three forms: the heavenly God, the physical God on earth, Jesus, and the Spiritual God. God's spiritual presence fills this entire space and every pore of at least my body, if not in the entire community assembled there.

The service lasts an hour, most of which is spoken either in Portuguese or Latin. It is a powerful and impressive service. Part of the service is done by a special South American assembly of 24 men, the Knights of the Holy Sepulchre, the keeper of the flame in the New World.

Commenting on the flame ceremony Lois says, "How very insignificant I felt as we filed past the honor guard and the archbishop into this magnificent cathedral. Yet how honored to even be here in this beautiful place holding our lamp in honor of Christ."

After the service, we are shown the special monument of three praying hands with their fingertips touching together pointing upward. It is 15 feet high and holds the Millennium Odyssey Rally lamp, with the Holy Bic-lit flame, on a gold chain in the middle of the hands. Needless to say we rally folks are feeling a little uncomfortable about the source of this special flame that we have provided.

After a short dedication service of the lamp holders, we are led into a fellowship hall where we mingle with the 60-some church priests. The Knights of the Holy Sepulchre and the sisters who serve the church are also in attendance.

Lois is carrying our still-lighted lamp and has an unusual and somewhat unsettling experience. First one and then another older, frail looking sister of the order reach out and touch her lamp. They speak a short statement in Portuguese and then grasp the protective lid over the chimney of the lamp. Lois does not understand the words, but it seems to her that maybe they want her lamp and that soon it might be snatched from her grasp.

She moves close to my side, but then notices that after touching the lamp, they rub their thumb or finger on their face and mark themselves with the black soot that forms on the bottom of the chimney cap. We are aghast for several moments, but then we realize that they are now bearing a mark from the tomb of their Lord Jesus Christ. We see this gesture as a testimony to their belief in almighty God, and we are humbled and honored to be able to participate in a small way.

The special flame ceremony completed, we cast off our lines, and head once again out to sea. We do not have a very good start as we depart the vast bay even with our extra crew. We are all looking back over our shoulders at the massive yet serene statue of Jesus on the mountaintop with his outstretched arms seeming to beckon us to come back.

The first day at sea finds us sailing nicely southward on placid waters helped by a warm breeze from off shore. Ken, as he always seems to be able to do, spots a large whale surfacing nearby just before sunset. Always a fun way to start a voyage, and it leads us into a beautiful night of smooth sailing under a starry, bright sky.

Unfortunately the fine sailing weather only lasts for a day and a night and then it turns ugly, real ugly. The wind turns south in the afternoon of our second day at sea. At first it is only 10 to 12 knots strong, but by nightfall it increases to 20.

By Lois's morning watch the winds are blowing 25 with higher gusts. The bow is now pointed southeast and is plunging up and down in the waves as they pass under us and our speed forward is now reduced to three. As Ken comes on watch at 10 a.m., the winds are howling at 30-plus knots and the waves are getting a bit large. Our headway is now about two knots so we start the engine and motor slowly ahead to help our boat struggle ever forward.

All day with the engine running at only 1,800 revolutions per minute, we can maintain three knots again. We cannot go any faster for the bow of the boat starts to jump out of the back of the passing wave and plunges sharply down into the trough of the next wave. When we take this speedy plunge, the bow smacks into the front of the next wave slamming into it loudly. It feels like we are running into something very hard. A grand spray of salty water cascades from bow to stern and head to toe over the boat and us.

By nightfall we reduce the mainsail to one third of its size. The big head sail is completely furled in and only the very small staysail is up. So with reduced sail area and the motor slowly assisting our progress we bash ever slowly south on a dark and stormy sea—now with very steep 15-foot waves.

It's great to have Ken aboard to cut down on our time on watch. He does not get seasick. He is good company. Yet another medical emergency ensues.

He was coming off his watch at midnight and was trying to get his wet pants off before turning into his bunk. He was standing in the galley on one foot pulling his wet pants off with both hands. He was, of course, bent over as well to grasp the cuff of one pant leg when an extra big wave suddenly caused the boat to roll to port, so did Ken, head first.

Ken's head bangs sharply against the same stove that caused our first medical emergency. Gamely he struggles to get back up even with his pants around his knees and with one hand covering his forehead. Blood is leaking profusely between his fingers.

I take one look at the bloody gash in his head and quickly return to my urgent duties on deck. Lois remains calm and quickly gets our first aid kit out of the forward head. She gets Ken to lie down in his aft stateroom where she can clean his head up better.

Lois finds a butterfly bandage and is in the process of applying it to his noggin when the boat is hit by what some would call a rogue wave. The boat lurches upward and then falls over onto its port side.

The entire top of the onrushing wave sweeps across our deck at least three feet high. It smashes into our plastic windshield, blowing out the fastener track on the starboard side and then cascades into the cockpit. On the way to the cockpit it rushes down the open window that Lois had opened to get some fresh air for Ken in the aft bunk. He gets fresh air alright and also a saltwater soaking of his head and upper half of his body.

I am thrown across the cockpit and only avoid going overboard when my chest bashes into the port side jib wench. Lois throws away the ruined soaked butterfly bandage, cleans the salt water off her patient and applies the last big butterfly to Ken's head wound.

This guy is amazing for as bad as his head wound looks, he shrugs the incident off, snuggles into his half water-soaked bunk, and promptly goes to sleep.

The next morning as we check our progress, we find that we made only 28 miles toward our destination in Argentina in the past 24 hours. That's a new slow speed record for *Que Sera Sera.*

Shortly after noon on the third day in the storm-tossed sea, the winds begin to diminish slowly. It is none too soon for we were all worn out from lack of sleep and from always having to hang on to some solid point on the boat even while seated.

By nightfall the winds have diminished to 15 down from the previous night's 30 to 35. It is still a "hold on tight night" even while in our bunks, but after the midnight watch the seas become much more manageable. By morning we re-hoist the mainsail, turn off the motor and begin to sail directly south. Finally the seas subside, the sun appears for the first time in three days and we begin the immense job of drying out our soggy boat.

At last we arrive safely at the large, commercial harbor of Mar Del Plata. We are battered and bruised and one of us is a bit bloodied, but never did we think that we were in imminent danger on the raging sea.

Mar Del Plata, Argentina! What a perfect place to be, and to be here for Christmas and New Year's Eve, 1999, is truly memorable. The Argentine fishing fleet of over 300 big boats is waiting in port for the southern Atlantic season to open.

At first we thought that this huge assembly of fishing boats was the source of a very strong, offensive odor and an early morning loud, obnoxious sound. Later an Argentine family we had taken aboard shows us ,with great pride, their city's colony of sea lions just east of the fishing fleet. There must be at least one hundred big beasts, all of which come ashore to hang out and definitely to poop. We are impressed with their size and seeming tameness as they constantly swim alongside of us just barely under water. Fun to look at, but we chose not to stay long for the stench was overpowering.

We are located in a small marina affiliated with the huge Buenos Aires Yacht Club. Only six of the seven rally yachts get in for *Futuro's* keel is too deep and draws too much water.

Everyone we meet is friendly and can speak English well, but then the membership of the yacht club is upper class and better educated.

We find time between the several parties to do some serious grocery shopping for beef tenderloins which are not only economical, but known as some of the finest beef in the world. We left with a full freezer.

While we were in Mar Del Plata, a young couple and their daughter walk down the dock, and, for some reason, ask if they can come aboard and look at our boat. This is puzzling because all around us are several bigger and newer boats in our fleet. While aboard, they notice our collage of family pictures, and ask about the photos so naturally we tell them of the loss of our son, Ed.

We believe this meeting was a God-created moment. They tell us that they had lost their 23-year-old daughter in the same month we had lost Eddie. With watery eyes, we share our sadness, feeling each other's pain. Even though pain is present when we talk about our loss, it also helps to share with those that really understand.

During the weeks we spend in Argentina, we become close to a wonderful couple, Ricardo and Gladys Accinetti, who are docked near us. Discovering mutual birthdays, they bring gifts to Lois almost daily. We invite them to the huge flame ceremony held at the 95-year-old Catholic cathedral in the middle of the town square. When we arrive in a 1937 Ford coupe just like the one I had courted Lois in except this one has a GPS unit in the glove compartment, Ricardo and Gladys invite us to sit on the stage with them. It turns out he is the master of ceremonies. We laugh because Ricardo had dressed down not to embarrass the very casual sailors and we are all dressed up in suits and ties.

Our rally group celebrates both Christmas and New Year's here with big parties. We are thrilled to see all the Christmas decorations while the temperature in the city is over 100 degrees.

We accept a bouquet of roses from Ricardo and Gladys with instructions to scatter the petals on the ocean breeze celebrating Eddie's life and our new friendship. It is difficult to say goodbye. We feel a mixture of emotions, of embracing and letting go, because we know when we reach the Falkland Islands, we will meet others that will become special to us also.

6

Argentina to the Falklands

We are looking forward to sailing to Chile and the Beagle Channel, but not before celebrating at a bon voyage party given by our many friends at the Yacht Club Argentino. We will always remember their gracious hospitality fondly.

Our rally start takes place directly in front of the downtown casino area two miles north of the yacht club. The starting line is set only 100 yards off the shore, and we can clearly see the several hundred citizens lined up to watch our seven boat start.

We believe, this time, we sailed across the starting line first with *Risqué* only a few yards behind us. It is a rough sea in which we are starting with six to eight foot waves coming toward us as we sail south-southeast. Even in these rough conditions several spectator sailboats follow along with us. One small wooden boat is manned by three of our new Argentine friends. We slow to let them approach. Then with friendly waves, and a blast of our brass horn we say farewell and sail away.

There are three of us aboard. Our friend, Hank Stein, flew in to help us get across this piece of often-stormy water to the Falklands. Three on board is good because we now have three hours on watch and six off rather than our normal six and six watches.

The next morning no other sails are in sight, but after receiving our morning SSB radio position reports, we know that our friends on *Harmonie* are only about 12 miles directly ahead of us. The winds are now blowing at eight to ten knots from the northwest so we hoist our big spinnaker and head off to catch them.

With our big 1,200 square foot spinnaker, we are able to increase our speed from four knots to six plus and by three o'clock in the afternoon we have *Harmonie* in sight. By 8 p.m. they are a couple of miles behind us, and we have a fun evening talking on our VHF radio with Ralph and Ann.

As darkness falls we take down the big sail, hoist our main and jib, and promptly slow down to our normal four knots. *Harmonie* must have done five knots, for by sunrise she is out of sight somewhere ahead. We still have the same breeze from astern so we hoist the black, yellow, and white kite and once again take off to catch up. This we did by noon, and by dark we are eight miles ahead once again.

This catch up during the day and falling behind at night goes on for six days. Each evening as we report our positions to rally control, we are within a few miles of each other and sometimes side by side. Rally control calls us the catamaran boats for we seem to be connected to each other.

We certainly did not expect to be able to sail even a couple of days down wind, so it is extraordinary to have this wind continue for seven days straight. Normally every two to three days a fast-moving low moves up from around the southern tip of South America bringing with it strong, cold southwest winds. We are lucky, due to the good following winds, and our big spinnaker; we finish third on this leg.

The harbor at Port Stanley is situated in a very well protected bay, and is full of historic bygone era square-rigged sailing ships that have been abandoned. We actually tie up to the stern half of an old wooden sailing ship that has been turned into a warehouse and dock.

We tour the east island and met several Falkland Islanders. They tell us how it is to live, work, and play on these remote islands in the southern sea. They describe the many shipping events that shaped the early days of the area, the bounty of fish and sea life that is so abundant surrounding the islands, and the hardship that the Argentine invasion and occupation in 1979 has caused them. There are still thousands of plastic undiscovered land mines in several locations on the island.

Our rally flame ceremony here is well-attended. Lois lights the lamp of peace with the governor of this once war-torn country.

Generally we have a pleasant time in Port Stanley, but we are all ready to get under way for Patagonia. The city has arranged a big send off for us. Our rally will be the first-ever sailboat race to begin in the Falklands. Even though we are sailing on a Thursday, the schools, the bank, several stores, and the post office are closed, allowing most of the people of the town to be present to watch our departure.

As we mill about waiting for the starting signal, we are surprised by a thundering blast fired from a large, old naval cannon. We saw this old cannon in the city park but none of us knew that it was still in working order.

The cannon booms once again at the start. The wind fills in from the opposite direction, and we make all haste to get our sails trimmed in for the new wind. Shortly after we cross the starting line, two Royal Air Force Harrier jets streak by over our mast tops. What a send off—the oldest form of transportation with the newest form flying over it.

We have a young Falkland Island couple, who had hosted us at their house for dinner one evening, plus another couple from Australia, plus Hank, on board for the start. With all that crew, we thought that we would be able to beat *Risqué* over the starting line. I'm sure we would have, but we were rigging our down wind sail when the wind changed direction. In the confusion *Risqué* just squeaked over ahead of us by less than a couple of hundred feet, but we weren't the last across.

We stop in a little bay just outside the harbor because we have to wait another day to pick up friends, Roland and Phoebe Van Rijn from Vermilion, Ohio, and to send Hank out on a flight. We drop anchor off the white sandy beach, and watch the penguins swim all about us.

The mention of penguins reminds me of our visit to the penguin rookery the night Roland and Phoebe arrived. After dark we hire a taxi to take us out to the beach to see the Jackass (Magellanic) penguins.

The penguins number in the hundreds here on this large sand dune. They burrow holes about three feet deep in which they raise their young. The adults stand outside the burrows in groups of three to four, shoulder to shoulder and keep watch all the while making a dreadful sound, similar to a large jackass. "Hee haw!"

We spend a few minutes walking through a few of the little fellows listening to their constant "hee haws." They are about 24 inches tall, so we are towering over them, but they don't give way as we pass.

They keep a careful big beady eye on us, only one eye for they never look straight at any of us, but rather turn their head away, apparently because we are too scary or too weird looking to look at with both eyes at the same time.

The next morning we depart at 4 a.m. for Chile. As we clear the island, we find plenty of wind and a big sea running toward us. After five hours of bashing into the heavy seas, and after our two new passengers get seasick, we find a westerly running bay and get into calmer waters.

We not only find calm waters, but also a very large British Navy ship in the harbor. We try to drop anchor on the opposite side of the harbor away from the ship, but while still attempting to get the anchor to hold, we get a radio call from a commercial fueling ship telling us to come over and tie alongside of it.

A short time later we are pulling in behind the Navy ship where we are led to a nice, long floating dock. Once tied up we are shown to the military quarters located there and given permission to use the facility. Our two female crew mates take advantage of the clean, hot showers the next morning, much to the surprise of the Gurkha Indian military men stationed there.

We depart the next morning, after getting the women out of the showers, but are told that the Navy ship is leaving at 10 and that we will have to delay our departure until it clears the harbor.

Much to our surprise, as the big ship departs the dock, two Navy aircraft again flew over, but this time they had a much higher craft to fly over than our little sail boat. The Falkland Islanders certainly do know how to give a sailor a rousing send off.

After a couple hours of motoring along, we find a big bay with some calm water near the low shore. Ringing the stony shore was a heavy growth of kelp. This was our first experience with this southern ocean seaweed-like plant. It is a very thick-stemmed and rubbery plant that grows from the rocky bottom. It fans its broad leaves thickly out on the surface of the water like a leafy blanket.

The water is serene in the bay, but the wind still blows through the rigging hard enough to shake the mast vigorously which also makes sound sleeping through the noisy night impossible. We four sleep some, but it would be a stretch to call it a deep quality sleep. Yet all were up early, and so were the anchors and off we motorsail to far off Chile. The bow of *Que Sera Sera* is pointed to the southern most tip of the American continent—480 miles to the southwest.

This is an area of some of the most inclement weather in the world. Huge low pressure storms are created in Antarctica and come swirling north through the Le Marie Strait and the mountains of southernmost Chile.

Now out of the safety of the snug bay, we find almost no wind but rather very large seas left over from the past days' howling blow. This is not so good for without some breeze to push against our sails, the boat rolls from side to side as we motor west into the long rolling waves.

At two in the afternoon our Immersat C communication radio begins to buzz to notify us that we have a message. Lois, who is always hungry to hear from home, quickly opens the message. Our son, Fred, and our daughter-in-law, Shelly have just become proud parents of a baby boy. Oh joy! Roland breaks out a cigar for each of us and I pop the cork of the bottle of champagne that somehow had been smuggled through customs by Roland.

Word of our perilous position on the vast and stormy voyage must have been noted by our family and friends at Grace United Methodist Church for they began praying for us night and day. We know this to be true because we motored without a tumultuous wind the entire 480 miles to the entry to the Drake's Passage and the Beagle Channel while the rest of the fleet had 60 mile an hour winds and 50-foot seas and we arrived within 12 hours of the group who had left three days earlier.

7

Tierra Del Fuego

With much anticipation, we look forward to visiting the fabled southern most point of the inhabited world—Tierra del Fuego! We knew that it would be something special, but we envisioned a dark, cloudy almost inhospitable land. Well, it is special, but certainly not inhospitable but rather, beautiful in every sense. It far exceeded our most exalted expectations.

It does not seem wild or inhospitable as we motor westward into the entrance of the Beagle Channel, which is about 12 miles wide. As we approach the waterway, the high hills of Argentina appear in the north and the many large hilly islands of Chile rise in the south.

We are ready for a quiet night in a safe anchorage to catch up on our lost sleep as we have been sailing for three days and nights from the Falkland Islands. We soon find a snug bay on the north side of a small island with protection from the prevailing south and west winds.

Had we turned left and gone some 60 miles due south as we cleared the western end of this island the next morning, we would have been in the lee of the rocky island of Cape Horn by nightfall. We would have taken up the challenge, but luckily each boat must first check in with the Chilean Navy in Porto Williams to get a cruising permit for those most treacherous southern waters. Ah ha! We have an excuse not to go! Everyone knows the reputation of the wild and scary Cape Horn!

The channel becomes narrower and narrower the further west we travel, until by noon we have to squeeze through between two small low islands. As we approach the island to our north we notice that the stony beach is speckled with tall slender stones. But wait, some of the tall stones are jumping in the water. Penguins! There are several swimming along the beach ahead of us. We had all seen penguins in the Falklands, but this was our first sighting here in Patagonia.

By three in the afternoon we motor past the village of Porto Williams and into a small bay—more like the entrance to a small river. We tie up next to a 50-foot aluminum sailboat that is tied to a 250-foot WW II semi-sunken ammunition ship. This ship is the dock, meeting place, bar and restaurant for the Porto Williams Club Naval. The rally participants are waiting for us and we make good use of the club for yet another rousing rally party.

Porto Williams is Chile's most southern town as well as a Navy base with a population of just 600 people, mostly military families. The town is built on the side of the hill overlooking the big bay, so the view is great, but they do not have paved roads, and only just recently have they extended running water to houses.

Porto Williams doesn't have much of a grocery store, so we had to clear out the next day and motor 25 miles across the channel northwestward to Ushuaia, Argentina —a very large city considering we are at the tip of South America. Here we have a nice dinner in a restaurant overlooking the harbor and stock up with fresh vegetables and meat.

We return to Porto Williams the next day to get our cruising permit and have fuel brought to the boat. We had some 700 miles of the Chilean canals before us. The wind would be on our nose so we would be motoring to get to the next fuel stop. We would never make it with our tanks of 200 gallons.

I solve this dilemma when we find a big, blue, plastic barrel behind the Chilean Navy storehouse. I do a little fast talking and get one of the Navy radio operators to come with me to see if I can buy it. When Lieutenant Marco Vega sees what we are asking for he laughs out loud and says, "Don, I give you a special dispensation, you may have this barrel at no cost." It was an empty liquid detergent drum.

Porto Williams, Chile, has only one fuel station, which is Mobil Oil, by the way. We borrow a pickup truck and load an empty 55-gallon drum in the back of it, fill it half full, and drive it to the Porto Williams Club Naval.

The trick here is to get the drum off the truck without a ramp, then down a small ten-foot incline to the narrow wooden bridge over the water, a span of about 20 feet on to the foredeck of the ship. We are tied up to the far side of the ship down about eight or ten feet from the deck. That is good for they can stand the drum on end, run a hose down to the boat fill inlet, and siphon the fuel out of the drum into my tank. It is neat and clean with just a small wait while all this is accomplished. We are quite short of fuel so it took four trips to the fuel station to top up our tank plus the new blue barrel.

This free 30-gallon, big, blue barrel was to become important, for it saved our skin when we arrived in Port Eden 700 rough sea miles later with about 12 gallons left in our tanks.

Finally we are ready to leave. But when we ask permission to depart the next morning the Navy says, "No, there is too much wind in the channel." We were well monitored by the Chilean Navy.

Early the next day we set sail and speed off to the west past Ushuaia to Caleta Olla about 30 miles distant. When we arrive in the bay, to our delight, we find our good rally friends, Ralph and Ann, already at anchor.

This is fun for we rig our long stern lines from the boat to the shore to tie around a big boulder and set two bow anchors out in deeper waters. There were only two boats, but while doing this complex exercise there are five skippers involved to get the job done properly.

This was our first introduction on how to properly secure the boat in this wild, windy Patagonia. We have lines and anchors all over the little bay to be secure no matter from where the winds might howl; of course it is dead calm all night.

Next we try to dinghy up the creek to the foot of the glacier that is flowing through the mountain pass, but shortly we run aground. The water coming from the glacier is muddy, brown fresh water so you cannot see the bottom, even at a foot deep. The brown water is a surprise for the front of the glacier is very deep blue.

All crew members from both yachts go ashore, and walk up onto the low ridge, which is to be our protection if the winds blow from the west. It was easy walking for only low bushes and two-foot tall grass could stand up to the constant winds.

The next morning Ralph and Ann say goodbye as they head west and we head back to Porto Williams to take Roland and Phoebe to catch a plane back to Ohio.

Once back to Porto Williams and our ammunition ship dock, we check out the flights to Punta Arenas for our guests Roland and Phoebe and find there is a plane out two days later. The airport is just across the river from our dock.

When the time comes to depart, instead of hiring a cab, we load their entire luggage into the dinghy. Just imagine three people plus a tall pile of baggage being rowed across to the other side of the harbor in a seven-foot inflatable. We off-load from the dinghy, lug the stacks of luggage up the bank into the airport lobby. Roland and Phoebe soon take off, not on a 747, nor a 727, but more like a simple 7 aircraft. This was quite an accomplishment for the little plane with the vast amount of luggage onboard.

Now it is time for Lois and me to head west through the Beagle on our own. We have a late morning start and by 1 p.m. the wind is blowing in our faces at 25 knots so we find a small bay and drop two anchors. The winds die down by morning and we up anchor and motor quickly west. By noon we are once again passing Caleta Olla.

Not 15 minutes past the bay we see the channel turning gray ahead of us. At the bottom of the gray wall, the winds are beating water into froth. Here come the big, bad Racha winds that we had heard about, winds that pick dinghies up off the water and whirl them around as they blast them sideways back down the channel. We want no part of that, so we turn good old *Que Sera Sera* quickly around, gun the engine for all it is worth and head back to Caleta Olla with bare poles at nine knots with the help of the wind.

We did manage to stay ahead of the Racha winds and make it back into the protection of the bay and get one anchor down just as the maelstrom hits us. Phew! That was close, but after having dodged the blast it seems like good fun.

These blasts only last for a little while. Once the unequal distribution of temperatures become equal from west to east, all is calm. We could haul anchors and go a few miles further west, but no, we are going to stay put here just in case there is another blast yet to come. It seems like the prudent thing to do.

The next morning we travel west past two big fiords to the north side of us. If we had chosen to explore these fiords, we would have seen large calving glaciers. To the south the mountaintops have fresh snow each morning which, when the sun beams down in the afternoon, creates mile-long waterfalls tumbling down through the trees to the deep blue sea below.

That same afternoon as we are motoring west in Canal Occasion, we are looking for our evening anchorage. The chart shows Caleta Breaknach, a small cove between a big hillside to starboard and a lower hill to port. We keep turning right around the big hill, but find no cove to our port, yet we keep getting closer and closer to the steep stony walls.

The channel is getting smaller and smaller and yet no cove is showing up. Still further, still smaller until we were forced to slowly turn left. We begin to have doubts as to whether we have the right coordinates for the place when we see the low hillside to port part a little and in another 200 feet there appears the cove snug under the hillsides with room for two yachts. It is a good thing it was big enough for two, for there was another sailboat already at anchor.

We proceed to drop two bow anchors, one of them twice to get it to hold, and then back up to within 20 feet of the stony bank. Quickly we lower the dinghy and I row our floating polypropylene green line to shore to tie around a rock.

The secret is to tie the line to a rock higher than the high tide line so that line isn't six feet underwater in the morning when it is time to collect it. When the tide comes in and the line has been under water for several hours, it will be very slimy and slippery.

Picture the boat moving back out towards the anchor for it has a big chain trying to hang straight down from the bow. The dinghy is slipping backwards away from the rocks. The job gets done after some serious slip sliding.

After getting the boat secure, we have time to properly take in this snug little cove. Because there is a large rock outcropping between us and the other sailboat, we cannot see them; so it looks to us as if we are the only ones in the anchorage.

There is a small creek with a small two-foot waterfall in front of us about 60 feet away. If we look really hard, we can just make out the cascade or maybe the trickle of it. The place is so quiet and full of natural beauty that it surely is one of those close-to-heaven places.

Behind us are a couple of dozen bonsai shaped trees which are 12 feet high with their limbs all to one side and curved trunks. They look like plants right out of some upscale landscape nursery. This place is beautiful and serene.

The next morning as we are undoing all the ropes and taking up our anchors, the other sailboat slides out from behind the big rock and passes across our bow,

We wave, speak to one another in hushed tones across the water, commenting on what a beautiful cove we had the privilege to share. Then they continue on their way.

The German heavy cruiser, *Dresden,* hid out for a month in a similar anchorage at the end of the WW ll. That's how big and deep these inland waters are just 20 miles from our anchorage.

Three hours later we reach *Harmonie* on the VHF radio. They are 30 miles ahead of us by the water route, but only about 15 on a straight line. We talk to them to see where they will be in a couple of days. As we end our conversation another yacht breaks in and says that they are just five miles ahead of our position and that they were the boat in our cove last night.

We talk a little more and the other skipper tells us that he knows of a shortcut that we can take that will lead us to the western leg of the Straits of Magellan. After a quick look at the chart, we can see his suggested route, and although it is not approved by the Chilean Navy, and is not included in our cruising permit, we see that it will cut off three to four big days. He says if we will follow him, he will do it. You bet we will. But *Harmonie* is 15 miles past it already so they decide against turning back for the shortcut.

It is an interesting side trip, around several large islands, through a narrow, 60 foot wide, shallow gap, against the south-flowing current, but once past that, it was a beautiful four-hour adventure to the western half of the Straits of Magellan.

Because of that one little half day shortcut, we moved from one day behind *Harmonie* to two days ahead, and as the weather turns against them as they head up the straights it put us seven, maybe as many as nine days ahead, by the time they clear the western end of the straits.

We try to start early each morning before the west winds from up channel start to blow hard at us as we sail northwest. This early start would allow us to get off the straits when the winds start to kick up into the 20s or more. This day is not so bad, but as we motor along the north shore, we are constantly passing potential small bays that our cruising guide says would be good places to hide from the winds.

We are less than three miles from our selected bay, when off to starboard, we see what looks to be a really secure cove, but it is not mentioned in the guide. It looks so good that after a little discussion about its potential merits, we decide to venture in and have a look.

The entry is between two huge black rocks and the cove is only some 200 feet wide. It gets a little shallow as we enter, but we cross over a 12-foot shelf with ease so on through the narrow entrance we go.

After we clear the rocks, the bay opens up into an almost perfect circle, with 600 foot tall hills all around. Down the hill to the rear of the cove through the trees a waterfall cascades and to our left is another much smaller one coursing its way down the portside hill as well.

We drop our anchors in the very middle of this incredible pool and stand in awe as a rainbow created by the mists from the big waterfall fill our private place with its beauty. Here is one of the several places where we stand arm in arm and proclaim to each other that we are the luckiest unlucky people in the world, and it has to be that our son Ed is present to lead us to this heavenly place.

To keep the magic going as we motor in unusually calm waters westward the next day, we hear from *Happy Spirit*, which is ahead of us. They have seen whales in the channel near where we are. We thank them and sure enough we spot one spotting us. Spy hopping is when a whale comes partway out of the water and looks around. Well, this big guy does just that. He rises up partially out of the water, 100 yards from us and takes a look at our tiny boat. He must think us no threat for then he glides slowly parallel with us, happily spouting his white fountain skyward.

It is this same gentle day that we take time out to do a little exploring. We turn off the main channel into a small gap in the low hillside into a labyrinth of small islands most only 20 to 30 yards across.

They all have lush small, green trees maybe 20 feet high. Each time we pass an island there are three more behind it. Which way to go? Left? Right? After two or three of these confusing choices we decide that perhaps we should be prudent and retreat to the main channel. It was spectacular, but confusing, and we were probably wise to retreat before we got too far into the maze.

The next day we catch up with *Happy Spirit* just before dark. We leave the Straits of Magellan and turn northeast to head into the next more northerly running channel. We can now sail with the wind abeam. This is the first day in eight days that we can actually sail. We have too much wind so reef the main, but at least it is finally coming from a favorable direction.

When we pull into the big bay where *Happy Spirit* is, we find them tied to a huge steel-mooring buoy. The buoy is 12 feet across with a foot high ring in the middle. They actually have to pull the bow of the boat up to the edge of the float. Someone then must jump onto the float and take the line to the center ring to tie up. We, however, just pull up along side of the big, 60-foot, *Happy Spirit,* throw them our dock lines and raft up with them for the night.

It is in this next channel that we see our first half-sunken ship. Our chart book tells us that we will be passing a sunken ship, but it is still a surprise when we do, for this is a huge ship. The forward half is under water and only the stern half is visible. It had run aground in the late 1940s and was a 1920s design. It has a very shapely, rounded stern section sticking way up in the air, mooning all who pass by.

That isn't the only shipwreck we see. Only a few days later on a very rare morning with no wind at all as we motor north on a long, 15 mile, straight channel, we slowly approach what looks like a buoy. A little later it looks like a small fishing vessel, which later becomes a small ship at anchor in the middle of the channel. As we draw closer, the ship gets bigger and bigger and we become concerned about which side we should pass him on. A look at our chart book shows another shipwreck in this channel, but this ship looks properly afloat and on an even keel. It is just not moving.

When we draw abeam, no one is aboard and no steam is issuing forth from its smoke stack. A close look reveals it has many big holes in its hull sides. Cannon practice for the Chilean Navy, we learn later.

Other than the cannon holes it seems to be in fine shape. No rust, still some blue and red paint on the stack, and yet according to the chart it has been there since 1972, parked on a stone shoal in the middle of a mile-wide channel.

Later that day we enter a large cove with a small island on the east side of it. The island has a small, 60-foot long by 40-foot wide cove on its west side. We decide it looks good so we drop the bow anchor in 15 feet of water and back into the cove as far as we can and drop the stern anchor. It is a very pretty place with trees on both sides to block the wind. Great, but the bow anchor will not hold and after three tries we haul everything in and go deeper into the cove.

We drop the plow anchor, then the second bow anchor, which has a tag line with a float attached, and while backing up to drop the stern anchor the tag line attaches. Unfortunately it attaches itself to our prop. All was calm when we start to anchor, but just then the wind starts to pick up from the west. The plow then drags the second bow anchor now attached to our stern by the trip line and we are heading sideward toward the rocks. Throw out the stern anchor, throw out the grappling hook, and throw out the cook! No, not the cook, but everything else that might stop us from colliding with the rocky shore.

We meet the shore, but very gently for all the stuff we threw overboard takes hold as we make contact with the hard bottom below. What did it hold on to? Not the stony bottom, but rather the kelp that grows everywhere on the bottom.

Lois acts very quickly and gets out her wet suit and is headed overboard to free the prop so that we can back safely off the rocky ledge.

"Overboard into this frigid water? No way. Get back aboard. We will get out of here without doing that," I shout.

As it turns out that statement was a little overly optimistic for just ten minutes later I am swimming around in the frigid water looking at tiny little blue starfish while untangling the trip line that has tripped us up.

With the engine now operable, we start to pull up all of the iron stuff we had thrown over. Each anchor had gathered a grand harvest of kelp. Kelp is a very heavy stout broad-leafed seaweed. It's almost the consistency of rubber and the stems are a quarter of an inch in diameter. The only way to get it off the anchor is to cut it with a very sharp knife.

The water is cold, but lying on the deck reaching down over the side to hack repeatedly at the kelp tends to make one hot under the collar even while shivering from the briny deep immersion. We free the anchors, move into deeper water and drop both hooks into a deep hole in the middle of the bay away from the kelp.

To recover from such a stressful exercise we go below and light up our trusty diesel fireplace, open a box of fine Chilean red wine, pour a couple of goblets full and warm our exteriors by the heater as the wine warms our hearts.

Now we are heading northward up the channels and the winds

are light and we spend most of our time just motoring along with the tall mountains to starboard and the rugged rocky hilly islands to port. We are passing glaciated valleys, but the glaciers are hidden in the ever-present fog that shrouds them, yet they are close enough to feel the cold air descending into the channel below. This is truly a place of massive raw beauty.

Mention should be made about our first fueling stop since Porto Williams as we had been motoring for 11 straight days. The first opportunity was at Porto Eden. The rally organizers had made arrangements to have 21 55-gallon drums of diesel fuel shipped to this tiny village for the fleet. We are happy to have the fuel awaiting us, but we had to hand pump the fuel into our jerry cans and haul them back and forth in the dinghy to the boat at anchor.

Let us say that Porto Eden is not quite like the Eden in our mind's eye. Think of an early American frontier town of the Wild West complete with a boardwalk over the muddy terrain, and that would be more accurate.

A few days past Eden, we stop in a cove recommended by the cruising book as sheltered from all winds and with a good holding bottom without kelp. It turns out to be a most memorable one. We find a small cove at the head of a bay. We back *Que Sera Sera* into the little sandy beach, and drop the stern anchor in eight feet of water, pull ahead as far as our somewhat shortened stern line allows and drop our two bow anchors in 15 feet of water. We lower the dinghy over the gunnels and row the two big green lines to trees on the banks on each side of us.

In the morning with birds singing in the trees as the fog slowly lifts, we start to lift our anchors when, a few feet from our bow, a dolphin surfaces and gives us a look. Then shortly there are three swirling just 20 feet from us.

We watch them for a while, but we have to get underway so the engine is started. Surely that will scare them away. Sadly it does. I get in the dinghy and row over to untie our green line from the tree. On the way back to the boat, swoosh! they return, and one surfaces not five feet from the tip of my oar.

They continue to slowly swirl around the dinghy as I row to the other side of the cove to get the other line free. Back on the boat we start hoisting the anchor chain up with the very noisy windlass, which certainly would scare them away. But no, for even when we had all aboard and the engine is moving us forward, there they are actually leading us out of the cove and back into the channel, all the time splashing close to our bow.

After spending three weeks exploring this wild and beautiful country, how can we ever forget the strange and funny steamer ducks, the whale spy hopping us, and coasting along with harbor seals and penguins? Day after day we viewed the magnificent waterfalls tumbling down majestic mountain sides. Often brilliant starry nights lit the heavens above us. The peacefulness of our many secluded anchorages was a delight. We are leaving it now, but the seed is planted for a return sometime in the future.

We end our Patagonia adventure up the Valdiva River. Once again we tie *Que Sera Sera* to a dock, something we have not done since Mar Del Plata, Argentina, nearly two months past. We are now at a modern shipbuilding yard, Alwoplast, with a new hydraulic operated travel lift, a sail loft and floating docks for 20 yachts.

We have not seen this kind of marine facility since leaving Europe. We have returned to modern civilization and are relieved that this is where we plan to leave *Que Sera*. They will haul the boat out and go over it from stem to stern and keel to the top of the mast and then e-mail us pictures of all that needs to be repaired including the sails. We have no worries in regard to the boat being safe.

Having finished the Atlantic Ocean leg of our rally, we can take a break from life aboard ship and return home to Ohio. In a week we will fly home to see our new grandson, Nicholas James, for the first time and stay with our daughter's family. It will be fun to catch up on what's happening in their lives. We have the time because we need to wait for the four boats that sailed to Antarctica to deliver the flame to that continent. We will also reprovision with all our favorite foods and bring back more books.

We have formed so many memories and so many friendships with our fellow rally participants that will fill a lifetime. We will come back in three weeks to begin again an even longer sojourn across the Pacific Ocean to Australia. God willing, it will be filled with new wonders and experiences.

8

Departing Chile for the Fabled South Pacific

Our rally start is at the mouth of the river some eight miles south of the city of Valdivia where our fleet of seven yachts have been treated like royalty for the past two weeks. We parade south leaving our host marina of Awoplast in one long line. This is the first sailboat race start ever from Valdivia so there is much to-do. For starters we have an escort of local yachts following us as we parade south.

The rally coordinators have arranged for a large powerboat to act as our starting line committee boat, and it is on station as we reach the river entry into the peaceful Pacific. We all do a little jockeying for the best starting position knowing full well that the big and fast Swan *Risqué* with her experienced skipper and crew will take the start. But our little *Que Sera Sera* has always been close at hand when starting, so here we are once again in position to claim first as we cross the start. Our new strategy is to get so close to the committee boat that they cannot see if *Risqué* is over first. We did get quite close, but no bump was heard, nor was any protest flag hoisted, yet *Risqué* still claimed she crossed over before us.

The bulk of the fleet heads roughly west on the rhumb line directly towards Easter Island, our next scheduled stop, but along with *Happy Spirit,* we head on a more northerly course. By nightfall the fleet is scattered all about on a peaceful Pacific Ocean. As the stars appear we are like small corks bobbing slowly along on a gentle smooth surface under a sky so big there seems to be no limit to its vastness.

The first night at sea, especially this one, when we have so far to sail, is lonely. When the brilliant sun appears in the eastern sky in the morning, all around us is serenity, and the loneliness is replaced by joy at being yet again under sail chasing the soft sea breezes.

After three days and nights of constant motoring north and still not finding much of a current, we sight a large, dark shape several miles ahead of us. According to the GPS, the lump should become the island known in the western world as Robinson Crusoe Island. The lump grows larger by the hour, but it takes all day to arrive into the protected bay.

We are met by a small outboard boat with two young men aboard. One speaks fluent English and directs us to an area to drop anchor. This is a Chilean Island, and we do not have a permit from the Chilean Navy to visit here so we are a little concerned. They promptly ask to see our permit.

"Well," we stammer at the same time,"We don't have one." "Why are you stopping here then?" they ask. "We need fuel and food," is our hurried reply. "OK, you can stay. Do you want fresh lobsters? ""Sure," we shout simultaneously.

As darkness is descending upon us, they tell us that they will be back in the morning with customs, and after we clear in we can buy some lobsters. They leave us to enjoy a motionless moonlit evening at anchor behind the very high mountain that dominates the island.

At dawn we awake to find *Happy Spirit* is riding at anchor 200 feet astern. Soon the launch arrives with the customs and immigration people aboard. We worry about not having a permit to be here, but because we need fuel they quickly sign us in and we are free to come ashore. The launch drops off the officials and returns for us and our empty fuel jugs.

Once ashore, Lois finds a very small store where she can call home and I follow the fuel man to the Navy building. Here he opens a wire gate on the fence surrounding the two-storied Navy building, and in we go. The fuel man, who claims he is with the Chilean Navy, is not in uniform, but in old, dirty jeans, and an oily plaid shirt. His hair is long and tied in a ponytail behind his head, and he is smoking a big cigar. His appearance has me a bit worried.

Once in the retaining area, he begins to siphon the fuel from a 50-gallon barrel into my 6-gallon jerry cans by way of a rubber hose. This jerry can filling takes close to an hour and while smoke clearly rises into the air from the still burning cigar, no one appears from the Navy building. He siphons about 18 gallons of Navy fuel and I pay him $50 US for it. He even helps me haul the jerry cans back to the launch. After loading the fuel on *Que Sera Sera,* our young English-speaking launch operator comes alongside with five lobsters. We purchase a very much alive five-pounder for 20 bucks.

After another quiet night behind this fabled island where Alejandro Selkirk was the sole survivor of a ship wreck, the story of Robinson Crusoe is based on his experience here, we depart at daybreak for Easter Island. With the island still within sight, we sail through a huge pod of what appears to be very big dolphins. There must have been close to 100 of these bigger than normal black dolphins all just slowly milling around on all sides of the boat. We really like to watch the usual dolphin antics, jumps, spirals, and rapid bow wave riding, but this bunch must have been hunting because none of these dolphins come very close and none put on a show for us. Little did we know we were surrounded by the infamous pilot whales which have sunk many a sailboat.

We motor and sail for five days without finding the promised easterly winds. Our days are filled with necessary tasks: navigating, checking on equipment, making sure the batteries are topped off, sails mended if needed, making sure coolant and oil levels are correct. Each day I make at least 20 gallons of water so that we can take daily showers.

Twice a day we answer a roll call on our single sideband radio reporting our latitude and longitude. These are updated on the Internet so all at home know where we are on any given day.

While I take care of *Que Sera,* Lois takes care of me. She plans gourmet meals, bakes bread and makes English muffins. Often she played Betsy Ross mending our big US flag.

Then on the morning of April 1st a message comes over the Single Side Band Radio from *Risqué* far ahead of us that pilot whales have attacked them. They received ten heavy strikes against the hull in less than three minutes. They quickly turned on their generator and turned on the stereo system as loud as it would go. Having put on their life jackets, they jumped and hollered at the dark shapes surging below them. Something worked, for the pod left them as quickly as it had come without any noticeable damage.

After 12 wonderful days mostly under full sail, we make landfall at Easter Island. Most of the fleet have already departed for Pitcairn Island, but our friends, Ann and Ralph, on *Harmonie* are still there waiting for our arrival.

Here at Easter Island one must come in close to the beach to get onto a shallow 40-foot sandy shelf to drop anchor. A large, deep ocean swell flows into the anchorage, but not until it gets onto the ten foot ledge does it build up and begin to form breaking waves, which then rush in to bash themselves onto the rocky shore.

The 10-foot deep water is less than 100 feet off our bow, and the ragged black rocks are probably less than 200 feet; pretty scary we think, but we drop two anchors and let out plenty of line.

Ann of *Harmonie* has a list all prepared for us on how to check in, what to see, and where to shop for groceries. Soon after issuing us the list they up anchor, and head out after the rest of the fleet that had left early this morning. What great friends to have waited.

We are lucky, for not 20 minutes after our arrival, a small boat appears from behind the harbor break wall with the customs and immigration people aboard to clear us in. After the usual 20 minutes of filling out several forms, the officials depart, and we arrange with the boatman to come back and pick us up in a half hour.

Once we are loaded in the 18-foot open outboard motor boat, we begin a short 200-foot run into the harbor. To get in through the breakers, the skipper must first run hard right for 60 or 70 feet where the rollers coming in from the southern end of the island meet with the rollers coming around from the north side of the island. The joining of these two sets of rollers somehow keeps the wave from breaking quite so big in this area. The pilot then must time the north rollers to be able to turn diagonally left in between the next two incoming waves. He slows as the first wave passes under us and then accelerates to full speed to ride the front side of the next now-huge wave into the harbor entrance. Once into the entrance, he quickly dodges hard left behind the break wall and must come to a stop just before hitting the beach.

There awaiting our landing is a towering Moai statue hovering over us with its deep-set huge eyes watching our every move. It is interesting to be sure, but still quite spooky-looking.

Having cleared officialdom and the glowering island god, we saunter up the hill into the sizeable town to look for much-needed fresh fruits, vegetables, and of course the ATT phone building to make a call home.

After a couple of hours of shopping, we head back to the boat. We notice that the wind has now increased in intensity and is blowing directly into the anchorage. This is not good for now we see *Que Sera Sera* has swung around to face the wind and the stern is now very close to the shallow-breaking waters.

We find the launch operator and head out through the breakers to our home, and quickly climb aboard. The once gentle rollers are now six feet high breaking waves and our bow is plunging steeply into some of the bigger ones sending showers of sea water across the deck.

We must clear out so we call customs and immigration on our VHF radio, only to learn that we must come back ashore. So we call the harbor launch operator and he promptly comes back out. The launch operator picks me up and is very angry with his officials who say that they cannot come to the boat to clear us out. He slips easily into the harbor again, gives me an ear full about the lack of character of the officials, as he drops me off at the foot of the dark looming Moai.

It turns out to be a 20-minute walk to the government building and another 20 filling out the departure forms required before departure. Then I do the 20-minute hike back to the harbor to take the small boat back to *Que Sera Sera*. It is now 6:30 and he has gone to dinner. I am a little upset.

He does return shortly and rushes me back to the now jumping vessel. The engine is quickly brought to life and an all-out effort is made to hoist both anchors and to clear off the shallows into deeper calmer water. We get a well-reduced mainsail up, our trusty heavy staysail out, and we are under way. We are frustrated by the customs delays, tired, and very anxious about the increasing winds.

Dark comes early and fast and we are once again alone out on the big sea. These are the times that we remember our son, and so I go below and give the clapper of his bell several pulls. Lois offers up a prayer for Ed and our family back home. This is the "peaceful ocean" and the winds begin to die down so we have a pleasant night at sea after all. Still it would have been nice to spend just one full night sleeping at anchor in a quiet bay.

Seven days later we spot a green little shape out ahead, which should be Pitcairn Island. The wonders of GPS! To be able to find this speck of land, only eight square miles out in this vast ocean we are sailing upon. It grows in definition as we draw nearer. It is tall and steep- sided, green, and jungle-like in appearance. The cruising guide tells us that there is a bay on the southeast side with a small beach and a dinghy dock for going ashore. We get as close as we dare to the now solid rock shore. We see a dent perhaps, but certainly not a bay. Even in this close to land, the water is still over 60 feet deep and a very large sea swell is running in toward the island.

A small launch appears from behind a short concrete wall-like jetty and comes along side and says drop your anchor here. In water this deep our anchor chain is so heavy that if we stop in place and drop it over the side, it just piles up on the bottom on top of the anchor. This is usually not a good procedure if the wind comes up the boat moves backward and the chain just drags the anchor along with it. So we back up slowly as we let out the chain to try to lay it in a long line along the bottom—hoping that the anchor would find sand or clay or even rocks to dig into.

We anchor safely and Lois scampers into the bobbing launch and is taken into shore for a tour of the little island. I chose to stay with our bobbing and weaving boat just to watch over her.

Lois is gone for close to four hours. I spend most of that time watching the long swells rise up and hurl themselves against the unmovable sheer stone walls of the island. I also try to determine if there are just two tropic birds or a half dozen flying in and out of the high cliff face ledges. Lois finally returns with arm loads of fresh vegetables, two bunches of bananas, five of the biggest grapefruit that we have ever seen, and a very large fresh red snapper for our evening dinner. The island had shown her every hospitality possible and introduced her to almost everyone residing there—only 45 hearty souls.

With good breezes and sailing rapidly with our asymmetrical kite flying, we will be in Gambier Island with the fleet in four days, and we do have good breezes. Sure enough, in the early morning of the fourth day, land slowly emerges out of the water far ahead.

It takes most of the day to get into the reef, and among the many large islands that make up the whole of Gambier Atoll. We have been in VHF radio contact with the fleet and they are moving from the main anchorage to go for a picnic beach party at an island 12 miles further into the lagoon. Party? Here we come. So we change course, increase the now running engine rpms and make all speed ahead.

With our radio we are able to find where the reassembled fleet is located, and are led around and through the many coral reefs that protect a white, sandy beach where the party is in full swing.

So after 31 days, we once again rejoin five of our fleet vessels; *Happy Spirit* has yet to arrive. We are very happy to see all of our good sailing comrades, and once again to be able to stand on the firm earth rather than on a rolling boat deck. We all party hearty, but Lois and I are soon ready for a full night's uninterrupted sleep—our first in 31 nights.

The next morning we are talking to the crew of *Risqué,* our friends from Oconomowoc, Wisconsin, about the April 1st whale attack and we find out some very interesting facts. They were questioned, in great detail, by a marine biologist located here in Gambier regarding this incident. The biologist has been studying whales in this area for about three years and explained that *Risqué* was attacked by a pod of pilot whales. Pilot whales look just like a very large dolphin, but are darker in color and can be very aggressive. According to his report, there have been 12 whale attacks over the past ten years, three of which resulted in the sinking of the yachts. We had sailed with Bill Butler in 1992 who told us his previous boat had been attacked and sunk by a pod of similar whales in the eastern Pacific.

Our hearts flutter when we think back to the day we sailed through that big pod of what we wrongly thought were dolphins as we departed Robinson Crusoe Island. We certainly have reason to thank God that we were able to cross a very big piece of the peaceful Pacific and to arrive here safe and sound in this quiet, safe lagoon at Gambier Island in French Polynesia.

9

CRUISING THE TUAMOTU ISLANDS

We all party too much and leave the lagoon on Aukena Island a little too late to get back into the main anchorage at Mangareva Island before dark. Bad news for we will now have to weave through and around several shallow, hard coral ledges in the black of the night.

Jimmy Cornell leads the way with the other four yachts following behind. We are the last in line and the boat we are behind draws nine feet, while we only need six feet below us. Still it was scary, for here a bump in the night would be very dangerous indeed.

The next day we go ashore and do a little touring in the main town on Mangareva, Rikitea. It reminds us of a small south Florida town way back in the fifties. It is clean, lush with vegetation, and has small, jalousied-windowed homes with vegetable gardens on the shady side of the house.

We walk to a big, white church with lovely light blue trim on the hill overlooking the village. Upon arrival at the Cathedral of St. Michael, we admire a wood lattice canopy, all vine covered and lush with flower blossoms covering the side lawn, probably for weddings.

We inspect the inside of this elaborate church and find it to be adorned with large brightly polished mother of pearl shells displayed to look like flower bouquets adorning the beautiful altar. We also learn that a cruel, demanding priest organized the creation of this imposing Catholic church in the late 1800's. It is truly a monument to horror for the population dropped from 9,000 to 500 as they were forced, receiving little food, to construct the building. The priest virtually wiped out the entire native population of the island to build this church, which eventually no one would attend.

After a few nice days recovering here in the large protected bay, we departed traveling directly north for a day and a night to get into the next safe area of the Tuamotus. I must stress safe region, for a large area of these beautiful islands is off limits to cruisers, due to the atomic bomb testing done by the French government near Gambier. The many tests done in the sixties contaminated a large area, and many atolls are still off limits to all visitors. We were told that the fish might have several eyes and hairy scales, according to the local scuttlebutt.

We depart Gambier and after a two-day and one-night sail, arrive at a small, uninhabited atoll. The entry into the lagoon is large with the tide pouring out through the pass, making it easy to find the deep water. It took several minutes to buck the out-flowing water, but once inside, the water was calm and peaceful. The lagoon is almost round with a diameter of six to eight miles.

We drop anchor 100 yards off the shore of one of the palm tree-lined small islands that fringe the entire lagoon of Amanu Atoll. Two of the other rally yachts are already at anchor when we arrive, *Risqué* and *Futuro*.

Dinghies are launched, snorkel gear is gathered and off we all go to view the underwater wonders that are present inside the outer reef. It is beautiful. Though the little fish are many and varied and the coral is colorful, there are small, black-tipped sharks slowly circling us as we take in the ever-moving scene below. These three-to-four foot sharks are beautiful in coloring and very sleek in form. Even though we have been assured they will not bite humans, we still get little shivers of fear when they turn their smooth crescent noses toward us. We don't stay long.

As scary as the sharks were, so was our departure. As we leave by a narrow pass-through, the reef out into the deep sea beyond the water is so clear that 20 feet appears to be only five feet. As we depart, we think we are making a big mistake. It looks like we were going to go aground on the jagged coral under us, but the depth sounder never shows less than ten feet. The wind is calm and the sea slowly undulating under us as we motor all day to the next atoll.

Futuro and *Risqué* head north to another atoll that has a very large oyster farm. They hoped to purchase the choicest of black pearls that grew in the oysters, direct from the farmer at a reduced cost.

We carry on further west, past a large ocean-going cargo ship that appears to be at anchor. Not until we pass it can we see that it is sitting high and almost dry on a coral reef. We find out later that it has been there for five years—no one was hurt or lost, but surely the captain lost his license as well as his pride.

As we enter our next tropical island atoll, Ahunui, we pass a small village on the higher ground on the south side of the pass. Several men are working to replace the roof and windows of a small church that had blown away in the last typhoon. They pause to wave a welcome to us as we pass by—most probably surprised to see two boats entering their lagoon because this island is well off the normal cruising sailing path of French Polynesia.

We pass the village and drop anchor on the white sand bottom, about 15 feet deep. The bottom here has many dark spots which usually mean seaweed, but not until departing do we discover that it is not seaweed, but rather coral.

Once anchored, the four of us dinghy to the village. Three or four small children greet us as we arrive in the cove behind the village that serves as their small boat harbor and the swimming hole for the kids. Soon the four double to eight as we walk up the sandy path into town. By the time we arrive in the village, there are at least 15, five-to-twelve- year old youngsters gathering all around us, talking in their native language and we back to them in English. They show us their new health center and their schoolhouse building with several of the classrooms adorned with many colorful crayoned works of local kid art.

Our host kids parade the four of us white Yankees all around town, each wanting to hold our hands. Soon we have five or six small brown hands in each of our large white hands as we walk along the sandy paths of the little village. Lois and Ann organize some games to play in an empty grassy area and we all have a fun time in the afternoon sun.

Upon arrival back at the dinghy landing, we have at least 20 happy kids in tow; well they have us in tow, and Ann asks if anyone wants to see their sailboat. Only a few understand enough English, but the older ones who have learned some in school know enough to say yes instantly. Ralph, with the two ladies and four kids load into the dinghy, head out to *Harmonie* while I stay on shore with the rest of the waiting horde.

The visit to *Harmonie* was only to be ten minutes, but there is a little delay getting the first party off the boat and back in the dinghy. Ralph finally gets them back to the beach to pick up more of my gang of kids. We load six in, but as we turn the dinghy around to head back out to *Harmonie,* the four kids from the first trip jump back in the boat with Ralph so now there are ten *mostly* inside the dinghy. After hauling several of them out one side of the dinghy, while other laughing kids jump in the opposite side, we manage to get the proper number of new kids loaded and underway. I was still standing on the beach with my sides splitting from laughing at the experience as Ralph heads back to the boat. This goes on for almost an hour until all of the wonderful little village people have had a dinghy ride and a visit to the big sailboat.

The next evening *Risqué* and *Futuro* enter the lagoon and anchor between the village and us. We have a little welcome party for them aboard *Risqué,* and hear that the black pearl farmers do not accept American or any other credit cards as payment for their very low-priced select pearls. So being very low on American greenbacks they bought none. Wives and girlfriends will not be getting black pearls.

Oh my! What have we started? The next morning there are half a dozen of our fun-loving village kids swimming out to our four sailboats to visit. *Futuro* and *Risqué* welcome them aboard as they are now the closest to the village. It was fun to have them clamor aboard, but after they swarm the boats for two hours it was time for them to leave. The yacht crews try to get them to leave. No, that doesn't work for they learned on Ralph's dinghy how to jump over one side and to climb back in over the other side.

The next day as we prepare to leave, we hoist the anchor chain up until it is straight down below the bow and there it stops. Seeing that it was hooked on something more than a white sand bottom, L.J. Morgan from *Risqué* swims over with his face mask on and finds that we have our chain circled around a ten-foot tall coral column. He indicates the direction to motor around the column to unwrap ourselves. Once undone, up it comes and off we go past the little village with the fun-loving little kids and once more out to the open Pacific.

Futuro also has the same problem with their anchor chain, but with a bigger column that had broken off and fallen over the top of their chain. *Risqué* left the harbor and was under sail nearly five miles out when Chris on *Futuro* radios a call for help.

After returning to the lagoon, Chris and L.J dive with their scuba gear until their tanks emptied without being able to free the chain. They were about to cut off 50 feet of chain to free themselves when several men from the village row out to help. They proceed to free dive—no air tanks—about 18 feet down to release the chain by lifting the coral off. They are offered money for their successful efforts, but took none, just smiled their big gleaming white-toothed smiles, happy to be able to help.

So with a little help from our friends all are finally underway for that most romantic South Pacific destination—Papeete, Tahiti.

10

The String of Pearls

I believe "The String of Pearls" might be the wrong title for these Society Islands of the South Pacific. Polynesia should more accurately be called the "String of Diamonds and Emeralds." As we approach the island of Tahiti, the first emerald begins to rise out of the sea. Having just been to the Tuamotu Islands that lie barely above the water and are only visible within four miles, now, in contrast, we spot Tahiti 28 miles away, as it towers high above the azure waters. As we get nearer, it appears so lush with foliage that it resembles a rough-cut emerald in shape and color. It is almost triangular with a smaller island, Tahiti Iti, attached to it. Iti is a smaller matched emerald and is lush and dark green as well.

As we travel from island to each subsequent island, we discover that all are covered in beautiful foliage. Each island is an atoll with a barrier reef surrounding it. The water contained inside is so clear that it appears as if one is looking into the heart of a perfect diamond. Perhaps because of their thousands of miles of beautiful, white, sandy beaches, they are often called the string of pearls.

As we arrive in Papeete, the major port city of French Polynesia, we find it is a vibrant, welcoming city. A dock awaits us at the foot of the town, stern to, of course, but still a safe place to go ashore. This is our first dock in over a month and a half since we left Valdivia, Chile. Here we also reunite with the larger rally fleet yachts that have come through the Panama Canal.

We are glad to welcome the three boats we had crossed the Atlantic with in 1992. We are now a fleet of 48 boats, with over 150 fellow sailors. We are sad to hear that our friends, Ralf and Inge, on the yacht *Malsen* did not continue with the rally, but equally glad to welcome Hinano and Teva from Tahiti on their yacht *Prince Karl;* they will sail the rest of the trip with us.

Good friends from Ohio, Fred and Roberta Pryor, fly in to spend some time aboard with us. The four of us do a little island touring, attend a church on Sunday, and spend a lot of time in the wonderful outdoor market place. The market is almost a full city block in size and its many vendors sell everything from seafood to pigs. Here we discover hundreds of our favorite fresh vegetables and many new and different ones including rambutans.

Two of the rally participants, *Harmonie* and *Risqué*, hold a lamb roast on the dock one evening with all rally members invited. They borrow two charcoal rotisseries from the Tahiti Yacht Club and set them up on our dock just behind our yachts in the morning and start roasting two lambs. Tables are set up and rally participants bring many and varied delicious food items, plus Chilean and imported wine and other exotic fruit punch drinks.

The next day we gather for one of our most memorable flame lighting ceremonies yet. Jimmy Cornell's original dream for this rally was to spread hope, peace, and goodwill to every continent. At each stop on our voyage around the world, we pass on our flame from the Holy Sepulchre in Jerusalem. This will be the first flame ceremony with the whole combined fleet.

As usual our instructions are to meet in front of the church on the edge of town by 7 p.m. As we arrive, each of us has a lei of fresh flowers placed around our neck by a Tahitian Christian. We are then led into the church where all of our fleet members are ushered forward to the front of the sanctuary. The choir, standing in the loft above us, begins to sing. Then the congregation joins in. The whole church fills with wonderful music. Even without understanding the words, we are moved by the music which we have heard in our own churches many times before.

After the singing stops, Jimmy Cornell lights the lamps that we have given to the priest of the church. Then the lamps of the yachts that have just now joined the fleet are lit by a skipper from one of the lamps that had been lit at a previous ceremony. We aboard *Que Sera Sera* have the delightful pleasure to light the lamp of Charles and Saundra Gray of *Sea Gem* from Florida, indeed a pleasure, for we became friends with them in 1992 on our first rally.

Following the ceremony, we all return to our respective yachts carrying our lamps in a humble and thankful mood with those beautiful Tahitian songs still running through our minds. As we walk along, Lois has a special meeting with a Tahitian man holding a child who is obviously retarded. Though he speaks no English, the man expresses to Lois the importance of placing his child's hand on our lamp.

Lois continues to pray for that child and his father, for it seems to her she had encountered a man with all the faith of the woman in the Bible who touched Jesus' robe and was healed. Her prayer is that God healed this child also.

One of the most special evenings of our whole trip took place when our fellow sailors on *Risqué* and *Harmonie* hosted a big party on the waterfront. *Risqué* had hired a group to teach us the Tahitian dance. I am sorry to report the men never got their knees moving fast enough, and even though the women did a lot of interesting shaking, they never got going as fast as the Tahitians.

Next morning our yachts line up according to size for the big rally race start. *Que Sera Sera,* being the smallest, set sail first. Others start in 20-minute intervals.

Our next stop is Moorea, half-day sail away, and since we started first and were so fast, it was a surprise when *Risqué* and *Adventura lll* squeak in ahead of us.

Moorea is still an unspoiled, tropical island: high, rugged, and lush green with several completely protected bays with diamond clear water. It's truly a beautiful place and our favorite of the Society Islands. We spend two days anchored in one of the bays, slowing down after the bustling city of Papeete, and the parties there. The ever-present parties.

On we go to the next emerald, Huahine, which is really two jewels: Huahine Nui and Huahine Iti. We have to sail clear around to the west of the islands to find a pass through the barrier reef. We stay here three days while getting our headsail repaired.

Upon the return of our sail, we motor south for two hours inside the reef to Bourayne Bay. We drop anchor in 20 feet of water under the resort hotel situated on the top edge of the bluff. It appears to have been mostly blown away by a typhoon, for only the largest beams are still standing.

We have the bay to ourselves, and so enjoy being afloat in such a serene natural place. Natural until the sun starts to set and then as we look up to the hotel ruins, the beams begin to look more like the old gray bones of some large skeleton. The dying sun's rays cast long shadows on the remains and everything becomes very unnatural, even spooky.

Raiatea is only a few hours away, so we depart late the next morning, leaving the memory of the eerie remains behind us. Raiatea has a big pass on the east side, but as we enter, huge ocean rollers are breaking on the reefs on both sides of us as we cautiously proceed through the gap. Once safely into the lagoon, we arrive at the upscale Marina Apooiti which is a Moorings charter base. We tie stern in next to a large two-masted yacht from California, and find the shapely first mate aboard has a romantic connection with a man we know in Sandusky, Ohio. Small world.

From Raiatea we motor one hour north to a much smaller island, Tahaa, which is enclosed by the same barrier reef that surrounds Raiatea so that it seems like we are on a small inland lake.

After a restful night we are starting to hoist anchor, when we notice the sailboat closest to us starts to row out of the bay. Yes, row. The yacht is 37 feet and two young women are pulling on two long oars. We ask if they want a tow. "No, we will be fine," is the answer in very good English.

"Where are you going?" we ask. "The start of the race today is at Marina Apooiti," the skipper at the helm replies.

I ask, "Why don't you motor over?"

"We took off the propeller yesterday so we can't motor," is his reply.

We take them in tow; despite their rowing efforts, they are still within 70 yards of us. Being good Samaritans we tow them all the way back from whence we had come the day before.

The next jewel ahead is the fabled Bora Bora. Upon arrival rally control directs us to proceed to the Bora Bora Yacht Club to pick up a mooring buoy in front of the club. We pick up a mooring, but when we back down on it to test its soundness, we end up towing it backwards until our boat is close to another rally yacht. Good thing we checked it out for three days later the anchorage saw winds of 25 knots and we would not have been aboard if it had dragged.

Once secure on a firm mooring, we dinghy ashore to visit the Bora Bora Yacht Club. It is not the normal yacht club. The palm frond thatched roof over a wooden floor with a few old wooden well-used tables scattered about reflect the native culture.

We wait here for a week while more of our rally fleet slowly enter the lagoon. We have been informally cruising since Tahiti, but from here to Tonga we will race as a combined fleet so all 44 are gathered here. We do some island touring and make our pilgrimage to historic, fabled Bloody Mary's restaurant several times. This is one of yachting's must-do destinations. In the Atlantic Ocean it is Peter's Café on the island of Horta in the Azores. In the Pacific it is Bloody Mary's on Bora Bora.

Even though Bloody Mary's had been destroyed three times by typhoons over the years, it is still a magical place. The floor is white sand, and the tables are made of big cross-cut trees. The seats are palm tree logs sanded smooth and varnished. The bar is a fine golden-varnished wood. The food is fresh and as fine as would be found in New York or San Francisco. Both Bloody Mary's and the yacht club's roofs are woven thatched palm fronds—less expensive to replace after typhoons.

The race start is set in the center of the lagoon so that each yacht can be seen under full sail by the islanders ashore. It's quite a sight. We had a glorious time at our last emerald island.

11

Lying and Cheating

Since Bora Bora is such a fun and beautiful island atoll, we regret that it is time to move onto the next tropical paradise. But we have yet another rally race start, and we love to race.

The start is in the center of the large lagoon on the western edge of Bora Bora. The starting line is marked by a local sailboat anchored at one end of the line and by a small blue plastic jug anchored on a light line at the other end. There are close to 30 racer types milling around downwind of the start when the starting horn blows, and we all head for the line which is up wind about a half mile away.

The big, fast yachts get across first, but then there are 10 more yachts of similar speed all heading for the line at the same time, each jockeying for position. The yacht *Jancriss* of Italy is squeezed so tight toward the floating blue jug that it runs it over. It must have caught on the rudder for it starts to drag along behind, much to the chagrin of those trying to round it to head back out of the lagoon. How does one cross the starting line when the damn thing keeps moving along under another yacht?

We all, sort of, crossed the now imaginary line and head for the pass through the reef and out to the Pacific. Several of the fleet hoist spinnakers and gennakers as we clear the reef and commence the largest ever, most colorful, if not the first, sailboat race to start from Bora Bora.

Because we are in the second big bunch of starters, we are in the thick of the fleet all afternoon with several yachts still in sight as night falls. As morning dawns brightly, the horizon is empty of all other yachts. All alone on a big ocean is just a little lonely. Single Side Band radio position reporting starts at 0900 and after a half hour of recording the positions of most of the fleet, we realize that although unseen, there are many yachts all around us, but just out of sight. We feel much better.

I record all of our close friends' boat positions at the 0900 report and also at the 1900 hrs report on special plotting pages that I purchased before departing Ohio. I also record those yachts in our cruising class number three group of about ten. I enjoy doing so for I can tell each day how much actual distance we have gone and then compare it to our nautical miles traveled.

This tracking, while reassuring us that others are still near, is also somewhat discouraging, for each day we lose more ground since almost all are faster than we are. They do have to give us time back each day, for the longer the length of the yacht, the more time they are penalized, so that in the end we should be equal. It usually is true except when motoring, and then we never do well. Rally control tells us that the handicap should be the same, but we motor at least two knots slower than our competitors.

This urge to keep track of our friends on the fast yacht *Risqué* leads me to also track four other yachts as well. The leaders of the go-fast fleet are made up of *Risqué, Taratoo, Company* and *Foxy Lady.*

After four days of plotting 14 yachts, something begins to look a little fishy, or should I say foxy? We had mostly light downwind breezes throughout our leg to Tonga, and so the fleet stays fairly close except for one yacht, *Foxy Lady,* which advances its position in the lead by 15 miles each night. Strange, for during the day between the 0900 report and the 1900 report, and when the wind is at its strongest, *Foxy Lady* gains little, if any, distance.

As I mentioned earlier, unlike a race, participants in a rally may use their engines. However, all motoring time while under way must be recorded. A rally participant may use his motor to charge his batteries without penalty. Motoring forward is penalized at least one and a half times, sometimes twice as much as sailing time. So motoring for one hour is reported as one and a half hours extra on the finishing time. If no other boats report motoring time, then motoring time is doubled.

If a boat motored at seven nautical miles an hour for three hours, while his competition was drifting along at three, he would have gained 12 miles. Yet if he reported his motoring hours he would be penalized four and a half hours.

This went on for the entire leg of the trip to Tonga until the last day and by that time *Foxy Lady* was so far in the lead that there was no way that they could be overtaken.

Further proof of the deceit arose when his vessel required 145 gallons of fuel from the fuel dock. Others used well under 100 gallons. How do we know how much fuel he used? He left his credit card at the fuel dock and it was returned to him by another rally sailor.

Sadly even though the rally organizer officials were apprised of the evidence, no action was taken and *Foxy Lady* was given the first place award for that leg, and several others as well, I might add.

After nine days at sea we see the Kingdom of Tonga rise out of the water, which was a welcome sight. The island of Tongatapu and its surrounding reef is huge, and it takes us three hours to pass by to the north of the reef to get into the entry pass on the west side of it.

We know where to enter the reef for rally control has arranged to have a Tonga Naval patrol boat anchored beside the entry. As we pass by the ship, we douse our colors to them as a sign of friendship. Seeing our courtesy, they sent a crewman scrambling from the forward wheelhouse to the stern to return the salute. By the time the crewman runs down two sets of stairways and back up one flight at the stern, we are well past them. We didn't receive a salute, but did have a good chuckle at their botched attempt. It's the thought that counts anyway.

Once through the pass, we motor a couple of miles to Atata Atoll. We are led through a very narrow channel in and around big coral heads and into a large anchorage where most of the fleet is riding at anchor in the calm, clear waters in front of a small resort. We spent five days at anchor in the lagoon, visiting the resort for evening get-togethers, touring the school of the little village on the island and attending an unforgettable church service at a little Methodist church.

Then we re-thread our way back out through the colorful coral heads into deeper water, and parade our way to the large main city of Nuku'alofa. Here we take on fuel and are able to stern tie to a high wall inside a well-protected harbor.

We await the arrival of our son, Fred, and his wife, Shelly, who are flying in bringing their six-month-old son, Nicholas, and our eight-year-old grandson, Nathan Coghlan. We have a little trouble getting them all out of the airport for Nathan does not have a return airplane ticket. They put Nathan and Fred in a caged-in holding area for over a half an hour. Fred finally slips Nate and himself out of the cage while other arriving guests of the fleet sailors are being questioned as well. He says as he jumps into the waiting taxi, "I may have done something bad back there, but they were going to send Nate back to Fiji to buy a ticket."

We are so glad to see our two grandsons. Nate would remain with us for 10 weeks and then fly home from Australia. We realize how much we missed our family and are so pleased to be able to share a part of our trip with Fred, Shelly and the two boys. And how lucky we are to hold our six-month-old grandson while he is still so little.

With our new crew aboard, we head north to the many hundreds of small islands. We stop several times to swim, explore, and snorkel over some of the most beautiful fish-laden coral reefs that we have seen yet.

As the sun rises after having motored north all night on a still calm sea, we look behind us to see that our towed dinghy is half deflated and full of water, looking like it will sink any minute.

Luckily big, strong son Fred is aboard because we have to stop and haul the dinghy up to the boat. We deflate the other good tube and hoist it back aboard on our foredeck. When we turn it over to determine the source of the air leak, we find two oval shaped holes the size of half dollars that look like they were cut cleanly with a serrated steak knife. What could have we run over to cause two similar holes but, spaced at an angle three feet apart?

That same day we spot a large whale off our port side spouting along in the same northerly direction we are heading. All aboard are excited to see it, but after only a few appearances it disappears. Not long after we catch a fine tuna so we eat well that night. We get to Vava'u the next day and anchor in a very sheltered bay.

Luckily we patched up the two small holes and had our dinghy launched in jig time so we were able to get to the party commencing there. After a reasonable time to mellow out, we started to talk about our various experiences on the trip up from Tongatapu. Lo and behold *Risque's* dinghy had also sunk during the same passage and was lost without a trace in the dark of the night. All they had in the morn was the tow line with the dinghy bow towing ring still attached.

To add some additional problems to this episode, it was not *Risque's* dinghy that was lost, but one that they had borrowed from *Harmonie.* A word of advice to all: never, I say never borrow a dinghy from another yacht; nothing but bad will come of it.

Going back a little, the yacht *Futuro* borrowed a dinghy from Jimmy Cornell in Antarctica, and it was destroyed by a leopard seal the very next day. Some say that rubber dinghies are sex objects through the eyes of a leopard seal.

Back at the pub we find that our dinghy definitely had been bitten by a shark, a cookie cutter shark. These are five-foot-long critters that have a small mouth with razor sharp little teeth that normally take bites out of whales.

One evening we attend an authentic Polynesian feast on one of the small islands. We sit down to a sumptuous feast with several of our rally friends under an open-sided palm frond-covered building. Everything had been cooking in an underground pit since noon, as is the island way. We are served morsels of delight, all wrapped in cooked, tender green leaves, and when unwrapped and placed upon the tongue, are wonderful. Even Nate, who doesn't like to try new things, ate everything passed to him. None of us had any idea what we were eating.

Every good thing must end, and so Fred and Shelly with little babe Nicholas fly home, but they leave behind Nate to voyage with us to Australia. Tonga is the first place in the world to greet the sunrise every day so we must be only halfway around.

Next we are headed on to the Fiji Islands. That probably will not be much of a sacrifice, but who knows what awaits us there.

12

The Race to Fiji

There is no rally race from Tonga to Fiji because it is an easy three-day sail. So we set off early the morning of June 25th in eight to ten knots of wind. Up goes our black, yellow and white spinnaker or kite and soon we are making five knots over the distance towards Fiji.

The wind dies at sunset and on comes Denny for the night. Motoring at night is good, for the constant droning of the engine hums the off watch to sleep. For the first time since Patagonia we have two off watchers, my mate, Lois, and our new crew member, Nate.

The next morning the winds from behind us pick up again and once more the kite is hoisted and all is good. Not for long though for Nate gets a little seasick and then the kite is trying to depart the boat. The head of the sail blows forward from the top of the mast and flies out over the deep, blue sea in front of us. As it is still attached to the sheet and the deck, it does not fly clear away, rather plunges into the water. This means with no sail up to catch the wind we slowly come to a stop. Once we are stopped, we go on deck and manually haul the heavy wet sail back onto the boat.

We are in the port of Suva only long enough to sign in, get fuel and fresh food, and to pick up our niece, Julia Papcke, who is flying in to meet us. We are lucky to get her aboard. Her cab driver, noticing that she is a very petite, brown-eyed beauty and that she is from America asks her to marry him. She declines his offer. He is insistent, stops the cab, but promptly Julia jumps out to catch the approaching bus. Safe at last! But only a few miles down the road a younger native Fijian sits down beside her and after only a few minutes in very bad broken English, he also proposes marriage to her. She does make it to the boat safely, still unmarried, and the next day we depart for the remote outer islands to the south.

Off we go to Bega Island and what a wonderful place it is. Not long after we lower our anchor in a large cove, two of the friendly islanders approach in a small wooden boat. One of the islanders is a six-foot-three dark-skinned man; the other is his daughter, a wee tiny five-year-old.

He introduces himself as Ben, welcomes us to his island, and asks us to come ashore to see his village. After a few minutes of talking with him, we invite him to come aboard, which he did with his pretty wee one under his arm. We might not have been as receptive as we were, had he not had his little girl with him.

He tells us that his full name is Veniame Vacėdre, that he is the assistant village chief, and that he will ask the chief to invite all of us ashore for a welcoming kava ceremony. All of us include Lois and me, Julie and Nate, Ralph and Ann of *Harmonie* and the seven Morgans of *Risqué.* After a half hour of visiting aboard, he says that he must go to the next village which is around the corner from our cove to see the chief, so he asks if he can leave his daughter with us. Of course we agree, but what a responsibility, the assistant chief's precious daughter.

Ben speaks very good English, but the little girl probably doesn't understand one word of what we are saying to her. Lois cooks her pancakes, gets out some crayons and books with pictures of whales and reef fish. She seems quite happy to be with us for the hour that her daddy is gone.

When he returns to pick her up, he invites us ashore to the kava ceremony at ten the next morning. "Oh and do you have any kava roots to present to the chief?" he asks. "Yes, we do," we answer. We had been advised by rally control that we should buy kava roots in Suva because it is the only way to get on these outer islands.

As none of us has ever attended a kava ceremony before, we are a little leery of what we might encounter. After drinking the kava, however, we report we will never forget this literally numbing experience.

The next morning we send Nate out in the dinghy to check out the shoreline for a good place to go ashore. He is gone, but not out of sight for 15 minutes when he comes back to *Que Sera* and asks if he can give a boy from the village a ride. Sure and off he goes. Soon he returns with Aporosa, an island boy about his size and so probably his age and introduces him to Lois and me. The two of them zing around the cove for the rest of the morning.

The adults head to the kava ceremony with the village chief. We all gather; usually no women attend, but we have some special women who don't want to miss anything. The gathering takes place in Ben's home with the 11 adults, the chief, an even bigger man who led the ceremony, and two other village men.

A kava drink is made from the roots of the kava plant. Kava roots look like the roots of a small pine tree. The roots are slender, brown, almost vine-looking things.

A wooden bowl-shaped container is set on woven palm frond mats laid on the floor, and water is put in it, followed by the kava roots. At first glance it looks as if they are putting the water in to wash them off, but no, only for the kava to soak up the water. Once the roots soak for a while, they are placed in a burlap bag, which one of the chief's helpers twists tightly. After several soaks in the water and twisting of the roots for 45 minutes, a small amount of grayish-looking liquid is produced in a wooden bowl.

Ben takes the first sip. We wonder if he does so to prove to the chief it is not poison. He did not drop over dead, but rather smiles with contentment as he swallows the fresh kava.

As all assembled clap their hands in a slow rhythmic beat, the coconut shell bowl is passed to each of us to take our sip of the offered cup. Not very sanitary. Not very inviting in appearance. Not very smooth on the tongue, my mate notices. But after about 15 minutes she also notices that she has lost the feeling in her tongue, and lips. Novocaine, she slurs, as she passes up the second opportunity to sip from the half coconut bowl of muddy kava.

The next day we snorkel over the abundant coral heads surrounding our anchorage. Our niece Julia is invited to go spear fishing with two native young men; she accepts, but while doing so, is approached to join them ashore for a romantic experience. She of course declines. The fishermen didn't catch the fair maiden, nor did they catch many fish either. The reason was clear, for as we snorkeled over the big coral heads we notice very few fish, and those we see are very small. Clearly there is some heavy over fishing going on here to feed the many families ashore.

That afternoon we visit the village and meet Ben's wife, Maria, and their two small children. While at Ben's house, the small children gather outside the open door and peep in at us. Ben invites them in and, after a half an hour, there are over a dozen smiling kids all respectfully sitting on the mat covered floor looking at us white folks.

After taking everyone's picture, we go outside to a nearby open field and Lois, Julie, Ann, Melissa, Zetty, and L.J. Morgan hold foot races and play the game "What Time Is It, Mr. Wolf?" with the 20 local kids that have now gathered. Surround Lois with kids and her gym teacher background re-emerges.

As we all head back to our dinghies, Ben asks us to come to his home for dinner that evening. We readily accept and ask what we could bring to help. All of us bring some food items with *Risqué* providing the meat for all.

Maria cooks everything on a small wood burning stove as we all sit on the palm frond mats on the floor. Ben holds everyone's attention as he tells us of his life in the village and how he went by boat to another far island to find and marry Maria. A fine meal is presented on paper plates provided by *Harmonie*, and all retire to their boats at anchor well after dark.

I should mention we made a small cash donation to Ben to help pay for a larger fiberglass fishing boat that he was having made in Suva. He had told us that he must go further out onto the edge of the reef to find fish and that he did not think his old leaky wooden boat would survive a storm if caught far out from shore.

The next day we wave goodbye to our new village friends who are all standing along the shoreline waving to us as we raise our anchors. With a last wave to our new friends, the fleet of three boats motors west for two hours toward a small, low island. Once there we all raft up together beside the uninhabited island. The island was still inside the barrier reef which is still another five miles further west. No wonder Ben needs a bigger, faster boat.

The day just happens to be the Fourth of July. Reason for another party, we all agree. All our U.S. flags are hoisted high, and we all are dressed in red, white and blue as we party aboard *Risqué.*

Hamburgers and hot dogs are soon cooking on the charcoal grills, a beer or two are consumed, and probably a little Mount Gay rum is swilled as well.

The next morning we all up anchor and motor an hour and a half west to find a pass through the fringing reef. *Risqué* leads the way, but has a difficult time finding the deep pass out to the sea.

The deep sea that surrounds the lagoon has six to seven foot rollers always moving along its surface, yet there is only calm water in the lagoon. On the east side of the lagoon is the big, high island of Bega. Visually sweeping all of the rest of the lagoon, no land is in sight. Maybe one could think of it as a lake surrounded by an underwater break wall. The break wall here is built with millions of year's worth of little skeletons of past coral animals.

Once through the elusive pass, the four yachts from America hoist sail and head off to our next destination—Musket Cove, Fiji. This is another world. As we enter a very well-protected cove surrounded on three sides by islands of white sand and palm trees, we see an anchorage area with dozens of mooring buoys and three resort hotels, a small plane airport, dive shops, water toys on the beach and tourists. We have just come from rural farming and fishing into big time commercialism.

Here at Musket Cove the prime minister of Fiji accepts the flame and lamp for all the islands. Young Nate acts as captain of the ship and asks the prime minister to sign our log book. As we continue to pass the flame to yet another country, the hope the flame represents is beginning to pry the grip of grief from our hearts also.

13

FIJI TO AUSTRALIA

The rally organizers want to put on a show for the tourists, so the fleet start is held only a quarter of a mile from the resort. Our niece, Julia, was supposed to fly back to Ohio, but because she has made so many friends, she decides to sail on to Vanuatu with us. That's fine with us for she is a good sailor, and will be a big help on this leg of three to four days. Nate is still aboard and just itching to get back out to sea away from the spunky six-year-old Italian girl, Ginevra, the only other child in the rally.

With this crack crew, we depart the dock early to get set for a fast start. With about 30 yachts all starting inside the small lagoon, we will need to be in a favorable position in clear air and not too near the reefs on either side. We set all sail, and start running the line to discern which tack will have the most favorable wind angle. We practice for at least a half hour before any of the other racers arrive. When the starting gun blasts, we are far to windward of the big bunch of yachts gathering close to the committee boat. We have clear air, and are already up to hull speed. What a great start—first over for sure. We are grinning big when rally control calls *Que Sera Sera* on the VHF radio. "You're over early, *Que Sera Sera*," control says, crushing our hopes.

Damn, no wonder there were no other boats near us; we had selected the wrong channel day-marker as the starboard side mark. In utter despair we tack about and head back to the starting line, now to be not the first over, but to be the last over.

We have good strong winds from abaft of the beam. The seas are rolling, and we take a big over-running wave into the cockpit. We sail fast for four days but the two youngsters of the crew don't feel very well for most of the voyage.

Note should be made here that when a wave crashes over the stern in the dark of the night and strikes a brightly lit laptop PC—bad things happen. The next day smoke is detected coming from the canvas computer carrying case. With great haste the $3,000 marine PC is unzipped from the bag and hurled over the side into the briny deep. Where there's smoke, there will soon be fire.

We finish in Port Villa at 0715 after having to motor in no wind for the last hour. We place well up in this big fleet on corrected time even though we had a bad start.

We spend a week in Port Villa, tied stern to a high wall once again. Our dock is right behind the village farmers' market. That is handy for each morning there is fresh produce displayed on the ground. It did have a small drawback. Each day village men gather at the edge of the wall, squat down on their haunches and spend the next hour looking down into our home. After watching our every move, one would leave to be replaced by another. The wall has a steel guardrail along it with vertical bars about eight inches apart so they gaze out from behind the vertical bars like prisoners in a cell. Strange, and we could not shut our main companion way for the temperature was at least 85 degrees.

Fortunately a fine restaurant pub is 50 yards away, so we spend lots of time there enjoying a little privacy and a cool drink in the shade. We eat dinner there often, for it is a fine British-owned and operated restaurant with good food and good service. The place we all meet for lunch is the California All-American sixties-style restaurant. Per Nate, lunch is the best meal of the day—real U.S. beef and American cheese-topped cheeseburgers, French fries, and coleslaw—even a cherry Coke.

The islands that make up the country of Vanuatu are scattered over 100 miles in a north and south direction. Vanuatu, the New Hebrides as they were known during WWII, was on the Allied path to drive the Japanese back to Japan.

The Allies, mostly Americans, built a huge airfield to handle planes carrying supplies, Quonset hut buildings, and many fortified ammunition bunkers. After the war was over, the Yanks offered to sell the bulldozers, road graders, jeeps, and tanks with plows that they had used to build the buildings and the airfield to the wealthy copra (coconut) plantation owners, mostly French and some Brits. The Allies didn't need the equipment anymore and didn't want to load it up and haul it to the US, so they made the plantation owners an offer that they couldn't refuse—25 cents on the dollar. But they did refuse. They would not pay anything for the equipment. They knew full well the Yanks were't going to load it back on ships, so why pay anything for what was obviously going to be left behind, they reasoned.

This rebuff didn't sit too well with the Army commander, and so a couple of weeks later he threw a big farewell party, and invited the plantation owners as well. The week before the party, he had taken all of the equipment to the top of the bluff overlooking the ocean where the party was to be held. After the party was well under way the commander had his troops start up the big bulldozers and push everything over the bluff and into the sea below. It has become an underwater junkyard dive site for scuba divers from all over the world to visit.

It was not too very much later that the native islanders rose up in rebellion, and drove all of the French and most of the English landowners off the island. Hence the name change from New Hebrides to the native name for the islands, Vanuatu, meaning "My Own Country."

Getting back to present day life aboard ship, our Julia falls in love with the very handsome crewman from the yacht *Taratoo*; Nate finds lots of native boys to play with and most importantly Lois is able to buy three jars of sweet pickle relish which she relishes, from our new friends at the All-American Restaurant.

From Port Villa we all leave for separate ways to cruise through the many islands to the north. We leave Julia here to fly home, and we make our way along slowly, visiting three outer islands before arriving at the fleet's next departure point, Espiritu Santo.

When we finally arrive in Espiritu Santo, which is a much larger city than Port Villa, most of our fleet is already at anchor there. We join a group of our rally friends having lunch at the Cow Fish restaurant. Here in Vanuatu a manatee is called a cow fish, which is certainly descriptive of those big creatures.

More and more of the rally vessels gather in the lagoon, as they gradually come from the outlying islands for the start to Australia. This gathering of the fleet in preparation of a long ocean voyage dramatizes the economic impact of dozens of foreign sailors arriving on these Pacific Island cities. A simple cause and effect is seen at the Cow Fish Restaurant. As an increasing number of sailors gather here for lunches and evening partying, the owners keep running out of food and beer. The last night we had at least 85 participating in the rally farewell party. In preparation for the party, they ordered several extra cases of beer. Because there was none left at the local beer distributor, they had to go to another island village to get more.

They made so much money during the week of our stay that the day after we left, the owners put the place up for sale and were moving back home to New Zealand.

Other businesses in town also feel the fleet's impact. The day of departure the grocery stores are emptied of most frozen meats and eggs. There is no fresh produce to be found anywhere, and of course there is no beer. I believe that even with the big cash windfall most of the town folks are happy to see the somewhat rowdy fleet depart.

After our start we have very light winds for the first 24 hours and so motor-sail until 10:30 a.m. the next day. We finally get a fair breeze and hang the kite up and start to sail at six plus knots toward Australia still 1,060 miles away. Young Nate has become an excellent crew member who stands two watches a day. He has from six to eight both in the a.m. and p.m.

As the winds continue to rise, so do the seas, and by the third day we are getting a little uncomfortable, with one of our crew getting a little ill. The skipper is happy, for after setting our sails in the wing and wing configuration, we are making good speed.

We enter the latitude and longitude off Grafton Pass' outer buoy into our GPS and are very focused on getting there with some light still in the sky. We want to be in the channel that allows us to safely cross the notorious Great Barrier Reef before dark. We don't make it, but the channel is so wide and our GPS is so accurate that we have no problem staying away from the treacherous coral on both sides of us. It's 14 miles through the pass to our next GPS way point where we make a course change of 80 degrees to the north. It is pitch black when we reach the turning point, and can see absolutely nothing, but we make the turn. Had we made the turn ten minutes too early, we would have crashed on a coral reef and been in great distress.

We continue north 30 miles along the coast of Australia through the night and finally find the harbor entry at Yorky's Knob as dawn is breaking. A long stressful night for the skipper, but we are rewarded for our efforts for we find a large modern marina.

We also find that Australian officialdom is awaiting our arrival as well. Immigration and then customs officials come aboard to check our papers, and to search for restricted products. Immigration goes smoothly, but customs is a different matter altogether.

A young woman in official dress wishes to inspect every last cubic inch of our yacht for food and plant products—anything made with dairy products, any kind of meat products, some spices and herbs, and even some wood products. She takes them all—even our frozen and canned meat. Worst of all was the chili that Lois had made up that very morning which she was about to heat up for our lunch. She dumps everything, including the about to be served chili, into two, big black plastic bags, and then hauls it all to her car.

The search and seizure didn't seem fair, but we are here safe and officially checked in. We are still fuming when she comes back to the boat. "Did I leave my car keys aboard your boat?" she asks. Lois fails to spot them, so the confiscator asks real sweetly if she can come and take a look. She looks and looks but does not find them. She finally surmises that she must have dropped them into one of the bags of our food. She could not remove the official numbered seal that she had placed on the bags so she had to go the marina phone and call officialdom for another set of keys. Ha! Ha!

14

The Great Barrier Reef

We were in Cairns, Australia two days when Nate's family arrives. We all are excited to see them arriving at the dock, but of course Nate is ecstatic. It is a wonderful reunion for it has been eight months since we have seen them, and ten weeks is a long time for Dee and Kev to be without their son.

Lois and I are ready for some time on land in a modern, English-speaking country, but first we need to explore the Great Barrier Reef with our family before we head into the rain forests of Queensland.

After seeing crocodiles and attending an Aboriginal Dreamtime show, it is time to fly to Sidney for a week. What fun to share this part of the trip with six-year-old Dean and three-year-old Ellen. Seeing kangaroos, koala bears, wombats and cockatoos in the park is not only a first for them, but also for us.

It is hard to say goodbye when it is time for our family to fly home. We feel so alone. Not only have we lost our wonderful, young crewman, but also we have separated from the southern fleet.

This small group of sailors has been our closest friends for a year and now they have left us to continue onto the next great cape, the Cape of Good Hope. The six boats will be joined by the rally participants who wish to deliver the flame to the Cocos Keeling, Mauritius, and South Africa. From there they will return to Brazil and the Caribbean. The six have been joined by two of the U.S. boats that started in Ft. Lauderdale and three that originated in Jerusalem. These boats will end the rally back in London.

We have joined those going into the Mediterranean by way of the Red Sea, and will finish the rally at the Vatican in Rome. Our desire is to spend two years sailing the Mediterranean when the rally is complete.

The Great Capes group had already departed for Darwin when we get back to the boat after our land touring. Others of our fleet had turned further south after leaving Vanuatu to approach Australia at Mackay near the Whitsundy Islands, and several would stay in New Zealand.

Before we leave Yorky's Knob Marina, we find an electronics service man, and have him install a 220 volt to 110 volt transformer on the boat for only Brazil has 110 volt electric service. While he is at it, we have him install a new battery charger because our original one has given up the ghost. We replace all of our stores which had been confiscated by that customs person, stock the wine cellar with good Australian wine, and set sail northwards, alone, to Darwin.

A fleet of 11 yachts are already in Darwin getting ready to set off on their route to South Africa, and we want to be there to give them a proper send off. Our fleet heading to the Mediterranean is not scheduled to depart for almost a month after the South African fleet so they are in no hurry to leave Cairns.

With the impending departure of that group looming, we have a tight schedule to get there for their send off party. So we make all haste to get underway. We are, however, sailing in the protection of the famed Great Barrier Reef. It is a very scenic area and warrants several stops.

This area reminds me of a shallow inland lake hundreds of miles long with an average width of 12 miles.. Clear water, white sandy islands scatter all about with afternoon breezes to keep us cool. The winds are calm every night and our anchorages behind palm tree-covered islands are beautiful and stress free, most of the time. Each day the Australian coast guard flies over and asks our flag, call sign, and last and next port. It makes us feel very safe.

Our first restful anchorage is behind Lizard Island. We aren't the only ones to know about its protected cove and scenic blue lagoon, for there are several yachts of all sizes at anchor when we arrive. After a stroll ashore, we find out why the island is famous. It seems way back in the early pioneer days in Australia, an English family living on the island for several years was attacked by the natives. In fear of her life, the mother loaded her two young children into a washtub and set off across the water to seek safety. Sadly, washtubs must not steer nor float very well, for she and her children were never heard from again.

Along the way as we travel further north, we arrive at a very small island, and find a vessel resembling a houseboat already in the anchorage. A man and a woman are sitting out on the little foredeck of the strange vessel so we putt-putt over and chat with them a little. It turns out that they are the owner-operators of a fuel barge. They are living on the barge as it slowly moves north with the lobster men. They offer to refuel us at a very reasonable price, but we have only been out three days and our fuel tanks are still nearly topped off.

The next day we are starting to get closer to the mainland because the reefs are slowly squeezing us toward shore. We spot an island with protection from the south winds at 1700 hours so head in behind it. This is a small island with a white, sandy beach, ever present palms blowing in the wind and calm waters close in. As I drop the anchor, Lois shouts, "Look there is a CROCODILE on the beach."

"Nah," I say as I glance quickly over my shoulder, "It's a log." "That's no log," she replies softly. Softly may be an understatement, but I look again and see that the log definitely has four legs and a long nose. The log must have been at least 15 feet long; no swimming this afternoon.

We are five miles from the mainland, and here is a BIG saltwater crock on OUR beach! We have done some wonderful snorkeling on several reefs en route on the Great Barrier Reef, but no more.

August 31st we are going to anchor early, so we find a shallow cove on the mainland and drop anchor. God works in strange ways. We had been at anchor for maybe an hour when a small outboard motor boat stops alongside us. In the boat are a father and his son in wet suits. The father is a really good-looking Anglo-Saxon man with his hairy chest exposed from his unzipped wet suit. Tan, too, he is. I think for a minute he is Sean Connery. Well, my mate is speechless, but I do manage a hello.

"Hi," he says, "Why are you anchored here when there is a large anchorage just around the point there?"

I explain that this is our wedding anniversary, and we are just very happy to be here in this beautiful place. With that he reaches into a big ice cooler, pulls out four beautiful, live, crayfish and hands them up to us, wishes us a happy anniversary, and away he goes around the point. With that gesture and those lobsters how could we not have a happy anniversary?

The next morning we motor around the point to give a thank you to our benefactor. As we round into a bay several times larger than the one we have been in, we see ten other big power boats at anchor. We pull in close to a 38-foot power boat that we are sure was our friend's boat for his outboard plus two others are tied on a long line behind the boat. They come on deck as we stop alongside, and we ask why so many boats are here. They tell us that they are schoolteachers from Mackay, and that they spend the summer up here catching lobsters to sell. Some of the bigger boats do it full time, but he says his whole family is aboard having what amounts to a two-month paid vacation by selling the lobsters they catch. Not bad work if you can get it.

The next day as we sail under our kite ever northward during the day we change our evening meal menu. We land a nice size wahoo fish.

After eight easy sailing days, anchoring in a cove or behind an island every night, we arrive at the northeastern tip of Australia and only 80 miles from the large island of Papua, New Guinea. We drop anchor just off the town wharf and ferry dock at Horn Island, which is across a narrow channel from Thursday Island. Thursday is a tourist destination, and the few docks they have are all taken.

The next morning after a quick trip to the village market, we depart westward to Darwin with a fair wind and a westward-flowing current of a knot and a half. For a few hours we sail on the Torres Strait and then the Gulf of Carpentaria, which is just under 400 miles long, east to west, and 300 miles wide to the south of us.

This could be a bad stretch in which to encounter a big blow from the south. We are lucky to be able to make real good speed using our kite and wing and wing. Even though we take two and a half days and two nights to cross the gulf, we do it without difficulty.

I plug in a way point for the Wessel Islands, one of which on our charts looks to have a fine sheltered cove, but we arrive in the early afternoon so press on across the Arafura Sea. The next morning we arrive at Melville Island where we turn south into Van Diemen Gulf, catch another favorable tide up the bay, and arrive in Darwin at 11 in the morning—five days after our departure from Thursday Island.

We anchor in a large estuary south of the main city center and just a quarter of a mile from our other rally friends who are in the city marina. We hit the tide wrong, and will not be able to lock up the ten feet until the tide is full. The next morning at nine we lock up into the marina and reunite with our friends of the southern fleet.

The rally organizers have put together a farewell party for the fleet of 14 yachts at the pub. It's a Viking costume party, and a burning rowboat, symbolic of a Viking funeral, is set on fire by the local club members and is sent afloat on the bay in the fleet's honor. This is a bittersweet gathering, for it is to be the last time we will spend with these friends we have sailed with for the past 12 months.

The next day three yachts at a time are locked down to the bay for the start, which will be off the commercial wharf a mile away. We are designated as the committee boat at the starting line, and are one of the last to be locked out. In the lock with us is rally yacht *Alperna II*, and its engine will not start. We pull *Que Sera* alongside, lash the two boats together, tow the yacht out of the lock, and clear out to the starting line, I might add, because his fuel line is clogged with black sludge. We drop anchor at the starting line with *Alperna* still firmly attached.

The rally is about to start. *Alperna* is finally cast off, and away sail our fleet of sailing friends: *Harmonie, Risqué, Futuro, Happy Spirit,* and *Vegawind.*

As we sadly up anchor and head into the lock, our engine coughs, sputters and quits. We cannot start the engine to exit the lock. I work on the fuel flow and discover no flow. The filter is clogged with black sludge. Is it possible that we were contaminated by *Alprena's* bad fuel while they were next to us? After a half hour of slaving in the hot engine room I manage to get enough coughs out of the diesel engine to get back to our dock.

We are so sad to see our friends depart that we decide to take our leave as well. We fly home to the States for two weeks. This is quite a trip because we fly from Darwin to Sydney to Los Angeles to Miami to Ft. Myers, to spend four days with my parents, and then on to Ohio to check on our home, have our passports increased in size for they were totally filled, and squeeze in doctor and dentist appointments.

It was wonderful to see family and friends. We also check with Deana Yakkey's probation officers to see that she is continuing to give her speeches. She is traveling to all the boroughs of New York City, and now is on her own rather than under the social worker's guidance.

Before we left, however, we had the boat hauled out to be cleaned and the bottom painted. We arrange to have maintenance done on the engine and generator while we are gone. That works out well, for the day after our return, the yard put our floating home back in the water all shipshape and ready to go. We did go, but not very far. Rather than return to the city marina known as the duck pond, we go around the peninsula to the upscale Cullen Bay Marina.

Locking in and out of these marinas has to be timed just right in conjunction with the large tides. Our timing is good as we get out of the boatyard, which has to be one hour before high tide to one hour after high tide, but then after the three-hour trip around to the other marina we are too late to lock in.

No problem, for we just go to a small lagoon behind a large sandbar below the lock and drop anchor. We are there for a couple of hours when we see the Italian yacht, *Jancris*, from our rally heading our way. We try to call them on channel 16 on our VHF radio, but get no response. They are heading directly toward us, and we know that directly between our boat and their boat is the long underwater sandbar. They need to come around the south end of the sand bar to stay in deep water.

They soon stop. Not because they want to, however, but because they run full tilt at seven knots right onto the sand. We promptly head out to help them, however, it took the better part of an hour to travel back south to get around the sandbar, and back north to where they are stranded. Once into the main channel we go fast for the tide is rushing out at least three knots. That is good for us, bad for them, for by the time we get to them, their yacht is already healing to port by 15 degrees.

Eventually we have Alfredo, the skipper, get his main halyard attached to a long line and brought over to us, which we attach to our stern cleats. We haul on the halyard until we get *Jancris* laid over onto her starboard side. With all ahead full, we manage to get her bow heading towards deep water, but there it stops. She is now healed over at close to 30 degrees and two feet of her bottom is showing. Not a pretty position for an elegant lady to be in.

We stand nearby for a half an hour watching Alfredo circling around and around his stricken yacht taking photographs of the increasing exposure. With that sad scene in our minds, we go back to our anchorage to wait for the lock up.

Jancris finally did get off the sandbar, and we both lock up into another world. Here we find a futuristic, modern marina, and a fine floating dock. We have arrived. We are surrounded with upscale boutiques, fine restaurants, ships chandleries and a big super market for re-provisioning. This place would be very close to a cruising sailor's heaven if he had a lot of money.

Most of our new fleet of rally participants are here or are on their way here, so we begin making new friends. We did have some old friends here also. Charles and Saundra Gray of *Sea Gem*, with whom we had also sailed in Jimmy Cornell's Columbus 500 Rally, join us.

It's summer Downunder, so a party at the Darwin Sailing and Rowing Club is held outdoors on a wonderful palm-treed patio under the stars and constellations—one of which is the Southern Cross. It's also the middle of October, and time to set sail before the typhoon season begins. Our next stop, Indonesia, will truly be a different world than Australia, which is so much like the U.S.A.

As we start our next leg to Bali, we pass by a huge six-story-high olive-drab catamaran warship. This thing is so large that if it ran over us in between his two hulls it would clear our hull and only take off the top third of our mast. That would not be good at the 50 miles per hour speed that it travels, but we probably would not know what hit us.

The rally coordinators caution us to stay well to the south of Ashmore Island, which is directly on our lay line to Bali. Although it would normally be a fine stopover place, it is full of refugees from Timor. Also because the situation in East Timor is bad, rally officials tell us not to go there nor to Flores. We take the rally advice to heart.

We have a slow start with our new fleet companions, but are third across the line with our kite set and pulling at a blistering speed of two knots. *Stampede* and *Foxy Lady* cross only a few feet in front of us. Off we go to Bali.

15

DARWIN TO SINGAPORE

After a half an hour of drifting along down the estuary under a droopy kite, we finally douse it for lack of wind and turn on the iron jib. We have a long way to go and at two knots we will miss the rally party at Bali, our next destination 962 miles away. It is a good thing that we still have the big, blue barrel from Puerto Williams, Chile, aboard, and that we had filled it up before our departure from Darwin.

While we motor along for a couple of days, I'll describe some of our boat's equipment in more detail. Before we left Ohio we had read a lot about what type of equipment a cruising vessel should have and some not to have.

We installed a small seven-horse-power diesel engine. A 200-amp-per hour alternator is attached to the output shaft, and behind that is mounted a high pressure saltwater pump with an electric clutch. This system allows us to charge our batteries, all five of them rapidly, without running the main engine, which is 67 horsepower with a much smaller alternator. By engaging the high pressure pump while charging the batteries, we can make up to 20 gallons per hour of the finest, fresh drinking water imaginable. We normally only make 12 gallons per hour for it keeps the water pressure required below 900 psi, while reducing fuel consumption to about a quarter of a gallon per hour.

We charge our batteries at least five hours in every 24 hours in order to make at least 60 gallons of water per day. Lots of water per day means showers, drinking water, fresh water to do the dishes, and even water to wash the salt off the port lights and dodger lexan.

We have an electric autopilot that sucks up vast amounts of amps, a radar system, a refrigerator freezer, three GPS units, a radio, a single-side, band radio, a CD stereo system, a little TV and a VHF player, two laptop computers and an Immarsat communication system. This is our home, and so some comforts are to be expected.

Here is how our watch system works. Lois takes the first watch in the morning which starts at two or three a.m., let's say 0230 hrs. She is on watch six hours, or until I crawl out of the sack, but usually that's before nine in the morning. That's so she can fix our breakfast a little before lunch. After breakfast I'm responsible for keeping watch for a few hours until she fixes lunch. After lunch I usually take a short two-hour nap and then I'm on watch until she fixes dinner. We eat all of our fine meals in the cockpit together, no matter what the weather. There is always someone in the cockpit while underway aboard *Que Sera Sera.*

After dinner and Lois has done the dishes, she goes off watch and is usually sound asleep by eight. Then I have the night watch until 0230 hrs. the next morn. I must admit that not only do I have all of the right stuff on board to live in comfort, but I also have the right wife aboard to enjoy this sailing life.

The second day out we get a nice northeast breeze of up to 12 knots, so up goes the kite. We are sailing along with *Sea Gem* for a while, slowly getting well ahead of her. *Prinz Karl* is also sailing along with us and is staying neck and neck. The wind dies off by 1900 hrs., so on comes Denny for the night. The sea is calm, my mate is in deep sleep, and I'm playing Free Cell on the laptop in the cockpit in the dark of night.

We are still motoring on the third day with the full sun beating down on our boat when I find an oil leak on the top of the engine. After much time and a few cans of oil, I find that the mechanic in Darwin had not tightened the bolts on the valve cover.

Fixing the oil leak reminds me that on the first day while sailing, I needed to start the generator to charge the batteries, but it promptly stopped. After much fussing I found that the same mechanic had neglected to turn on the fuel feed hose valve at the filter.

We have been motoring all day, but later get a call on the VHF about 1500 hrs. from *Prinz Karl* that they have caught a big fish and if we will slow down they will pass some over to us. We slow and the tiny little Tahitian, Hinano, the first mate aboard *Prinz Karl,* has a plastic bag hanging on the end of a boat hook filled with several fillets of mahi mahi. We return some of their generosity with a bottle of our best Australian wine. What a fun diversion from the continuous motoring, and what a delicious fresh fish dinner we had.

We have gotten close to so many fine people, and over time, we have shared the reason we joined the rally. We find out that Robin from Britain has also lost not one, but two of his daughters, one in a skiing accident and the other took her own life out of grief. When he heard of the pain we are carrying with us, he gave us a poem that has helped him. One of the lines in the poem reads, "I am the sparkle on the water."

Lois often remarks about the sparkles to me as we sail along on a sea full of diamond-like sparkles. The sparkles in the day created by the sun, and the sparkles at night caused by the phosphorescence in the water, keep Ed with us.

The evening of our fifth day at sea, we hoist the kite in 12 knots of fair breeze. We seldom fly the kite at night, but we have motored for four straight days so we let it pull us through most of the night. We finally motor into the Bali Yacht Club harbor at 10:45 in the morning with a near empty fuel tank. Thank goodness that we have the extra 35 gallons in the blue barrel. It has served us well all across the Pacific. Now, however, we take it off the deck and give it to a local man. We purchase five small jerry cans as a replacement, for we will not be traveling such long distances from here on.

Sailing friends, Tom and Frank Silva from Ft. Wayne, Indiana, have come aboard to join us on the trip to Singapore. Once they are aboard, we set off to the north. This is a cruising leg so there is no formal start.

Four days out we find some of our fleet at anchor off a small island with a big resort on a white, sandy beach. Now a big resort means a big fine restaurant, so we drop our hook and dinghy ashore to join them for lunch. At that moment, a rain squall with strong winds races over the resort and soon someone comes in announcing that two of the boats at anchor are dragging, and one of them is ours. Frank and I jump into a motorboat from the resort and get back to *Que Sera Sera* quickly. The dear girl has not ventured too far. Only the small stern anchor drags and the main anchor is holding her fine head to the wind. Tom and Lois return shortly in our dinghy fully dressed in diving masks and snorkels for it is still raining heavily. We're out of here.

We don't go too far before we get a call from *Prinz Karl* that they have found a snug harbor behind the next island further north. We join them there and find *Nosey Be* and *Ginger* there as well. This fleet is to become inseparable for the balance of the voyage to Singapore.

The fleet of three French-built Amels, plus one, is the code name of our fleet as we motor—often sail—along our way to Singapore. We are within sight constantly, even slowing down to receive a bottle of French champagne from our friends on *Prinz Karl*. Why the champagne? We are going to cross from the southern hemisphere into the northern hemisphere during the night. In the early hours of November 6th we all cross the equator together at 0400 hours on a dark, calm night.

We actually stop with all four boats just milling around very close together. *Nosy Be* and *Ginger* shoot off some flares. We all turn on our spreader lights, I recite a little poem and Hinano of *Prinz Karl* sways to a Polynesian song on the foredeck dressed in a sarong from her native country of Tahiti. We stayed as if suspended over an invisible line in the water, for 20 minutes, all enjoying the event and each others' company.

King Neptune appears on *Que Sera Sera* and our two pollywogs, Tom and Frank, are duly marked with bright, red nail polish dabbed on their big toes as we cross the equator. It was a good thing we crossed the equator that night, for the next three nights were full of rain.

As we approach the busiest shipping port in the world, Singapore, it is, of course, in the dark of the night. We are still all in a row heading across the shipping channel towards the shore. A steady stream of vessels of all sizes is heading both ways across our path.

We are the last of the four yachts, and have a vessel close behind with a very powerful white light shining directly at us. While keeping a close eye on what seems like an overtaking ship, the three Amels make a hard right turn and head across the channel. By the time I turn behind them, I see a large ship bearing down on the three from the west. I then turn quickly to port and take a parallel course well below the rapidly approaching ship.

It is very hard to judge speed and distance on such a dark night. The ships are well lit, but without land or even a cloud in the sky to relate to, it is very hard to determine their speed. The big ship passes by us with plenty of room to spare, but I, for one, was surely glad to see the morning sunrise.

Just before noon we arrive at the brand new Royal Singapore Yacht Club, and is it ever royal—floating docks with easy access to fuel, and a full- sized swimming pool set right in the middle of the club grounds. An elegant shower room awaits us, plus an attendant standing at the shower room door with a thick bath towel.

The rally organizers host a wine and beer party with a flame ceremony at the club. One of our yacht's skippers presents a brass rally lantern to the smartly dressed Yacht Club officers in attendance.

Singapore is a large modern city, and is very green with numerous parks and thousands of trees. As the Christmas season is fast approaching, we begin to see large colorful decorations in the big department stores, just as we would back in the U.S.A. No snow and never will be, for we are only a couple hundred miles north of the Equator.

Tom and Frank host Lois and me for dinner at the historic Raffles restaurant, and generally spoil us with generosity before they depart for home. This is an exciting city with an attractive mix of the old and the new. We do a little shopping since this is an English-speaking country that has everything money can buy. We didn't buy everything but we did manage to buy two beautiful silk Kashmiri rugs—one for the boat and a long elegant one for our home.

We attend a large Methodist church for the first time since Tonga where we give God our thanks for the safe journey. We catch our breath and prepare for the next leg of our voyage, one which we are very much looking forward to—Thailand.

16

Amazing Malaysia

It's not easy leaving beautiful Singapore, but time is rushing on. As we depart the marina, *Stampede* leads the way. Shipping traffic in the outer harbor is intense. The ring of islands to the west is loaded, from one end to the other, with oil refineries and the straits are filled with oil tankers. In the harbor there are immense container-loading gantries so that even before we get to the oil tankers we need to clear the multitude of container ships. There is a haze in the morning air, and the scene looks like an armada of war ships off Normandy on D-Day about to invade the Germans.

Our destination is the city of Port Klang in Malaysia. After sailing most of the morning, we are motoring northward on the Straits of Malacca. This strait is the funnel for all shipping between the Indian Ocean and the South China Sea. It is roughly 200 miles wide at the northern entry, narrowing down to less than 30 miles wide at its southern end.

The 900-mile long Indonesian island of Sumatra, looming off our port side, is well known as the home of many pirates. Every year even large ships are attacked along this channel; with that in mind we hug the coast of Malaysia.

Port Klang is ten miles up the Klang River where we anchor in dark, brown water among 40 other sailboats in front of the Port Klang Yacht Club. A big fleet is gathered here for the Raja Muda International Regatta. Our rally organizers urge us to enter this regatta for safety in numbers, and to ensure it, we are to be escorted by a Malaysian Navy patrol ship.

The Regatta has organized a bus trip for rally participants to visit the city of Kuala Lumpur. We hop on the bus the next morning to visit the largest city in Malaysia. We have just left the large, modern city of Singapore and expect Kuala Lumpur to be something less. Wrong. It is more. Upon entering the city, we have to blink our eyes to make sure we are not looking at New York City. It's a beautiful city with a blend of the old and of the new, and has the tallest building in the world, at the time—the Pelronas Twin Towers. We visit a superb new Muslim antiquities museum before boarding our bus for Port Klang.

The Yacht Club hosts a big send-off party for close to 300 people, on the two porches overlooking the yachts at anchor. It is beautifully presented, in the old club house building. The male attendees are very well dressed in suits and the ladies lovely in modern evening gowns. All is going well until a strong thunderstorm dampens the party when the porch roofs leak heavily.

Since our race start is not until 2 p.m., we have a leisurely morning aboard. When we do up anchor to depart, the chain comes up muddy and rusted. Every foot of chain that has lain on the mucky bottom is totally rusted. When we dropped it in it the water, it was gray coated with a galvanized layer to keep it from rusting. The galvanized protection is now gone and a solid layer of rust remains.

It takes me awhile to get the mud off the anchor chain. After some sightseeing, we proceed to the starting line at the mouth of the river. At least we think this is where the start is, but when we arrive the whole fleet is gathering four miles further north. We give our engine the gun, but are still ten minutes late for the starting gun.

Our first leg to Lumut is also the longest, some 84 miles as the crow flies. We quickly get the kite flying as we head out on the Straits of Malacca, and stay with most of our class of small cruising yachts, if just a little behind.

After a couple of good sailing hours, the sky to our stern is getting dark. Eight hours later, just to add to the seemingly stormy sky, nightfall descends upon us. A sailor hates to have a storm and darkness come upon him especially on the first night at sea. Lois must have sent up some powerful prayers as she went to bed, for although it was a dark starless night, neither storm nor even much wind overwhelms us.

At our normal sailing speed, we travel 120 nautical miles per 24 hours. We do a little better than that while motoring, and much better if we have the kite flying with winds above ten knots. In that we are only sailing 84 miles, this will be about a 15-hour sail to Lumut. The timing works out that this is mostly a night race.

An interesting sidelight to this race is that the Malaysian Navy boat calls each and every boat twice during the night to take our position and status. There are at least 50 yachts in the fleet. It takes close to five minutes for them to call and for each yacht to respond with its position. They start at 10 p.m., and call well past midnight. Each yacht has a registration number, and each is called in sequential number. Five minutes for 50 boats is four hours ten minutes. We must keep our VHF radios on all night listening while this chatter goes back and forth. We are used to being able to sleep during the off watch, but this is now impossible.

In broken English over the radio comes, "Boat number 27 this is Navy vessel *Big Sea;* do you read me?" Boat number 27 responds,"*Big Sea* this is vessel 27 *Stampede,* our position is, 03 degrees 45.397 minutes north and 100 degrees 51.503 minutes east; do you copy?"

"I copy *Stampede;* your position is 03 degrees 45.397 minutes north, 100 degrees 51.503 minutes east, correct?" "Roger, *Stampede* standing by."

Then *Big Sea* replies, "Victor Mike Tango, Victor Mike Tango." And this same scenario continues on and on throughout the night.

We are mostly motoring, but at 10:45 a nice breeze fills in and we set all sail. We continue to sail through the night and cross the finish line at 0612 in the morning, both of us very short on sleep. We motor up another river, this one with clear water, and drop our now rusty anchor and chain in front of the new modern Lumut Yacht Club, eat breakfast and go to bed. One day of recovery, then one night of send off partying, and off we go on the next leg of the race. The start is at noon, and we are heading to Penang only 67 nautical miles further north. Our fleet is the first fleet to start, and this time we are at the start on time, and sail over the line third, but going fast with our kite flying.

We sail every inch of this leg, even though we go from kite to a double-reefed mainsail in a short thunder storm, to drifting along in five knots or less zephyrs at the finish. We cross the finish line at one knot at 0320 hours. No sleep again and of course Victor Mike Tango makes his nightly calls to us all. We find a small island with a protected cove, and drop the hook and go directly to sleep.

Upon awakening with bleary eyes, we are surprised to find the beach in our cove full of people who have evidently spent the night there in tents. There are at least 100, who seem to us to be local Malaysians. But soon we realize they must be Muslims for several go into the water to swim fully clothed. We have seen enough Muslims clothed in robes, wraps, and full gowns to understand their religious custom of keeping their bodies covered, but it is still a surprise.

Penang is a large island with the large city of Georgetown located on the north end of the island. We leave our beach and motor the 12 miles up the fast out-flowing tide through the narrows between the island and the mainland. We arrive at our designated anchorage after noon and choose a small, open spot among the 40 yachts already at anchor. The tide is running at close to three knots so this is an iffy place to anchor, but it is the only place, so we drop two hooks just to be safe.

The next day we team up with Claus and Brigetta of the rally yacht *Ginger* and tour the city. What a city it is. Hovering high above the big downtown buildings is a huge Buddhist Temple, the Temple of Ten Thousand Buddhas. We spend at least three hours touring this vast architectural and religious wonder, learning firsthand about their religion. There are at least 10,000 Buddha statues in every shape, size, and color here. An amazing example was of the 12-foot high, hand-carved blue quartz twin Buddhas given to the Temple by the German government.

We also visit the huge Temple of the Reclining Buddha. It is the largest reclining Buddha in the world—99 feet of gold plated opulence. The entire interior of the temple is literally coated in gold. What an amazing place.

After spending three days at anchor in front of the city, it's time to start our last leg to the island of Langkawi, 60 miles north. We have yet another good kite start, and get a sizeable lead, but after an hour the big yachts all come sailing by us with their huge kites set and pulling. The first to pass us is *Stampede,* with her scarlet and gray setting the pace for the rest of the fleet. Great start, but by 1400 hrs. most of us are motoring in gentle zephyrs once again.

As we are sailing along at 1720 hrs. in the evening, a small outboard motorboat comes beside us and a young man and his wife offer to sell us fish. They cruise along beside us, and we do sign language back and forth to communicate. She holds up a couple of crabs and some small shrimp. With a head nod she agrees to our price. We get our boat hook, and pass her our plastic bucket with a US ten dollar bill inside. She takes the bill, and dumps in the seafood, all this time her husband is motoring along close behind us to keep pace with our three-knot speed. All of our faces are wreathed in big smiles as the two participants go their separate ways.

Back to night sailing again and Victor Mike Tango's endless radio calls. We arrive in the dark of the night at the anchorage off the Langkawi Yacht Club just after midnight.

The next day as we are reminiscing about the race with other sailors, Lois remarks about her lack of sleep because of *Big Sea's* constant repeating Victor Mike Tango all through the night. Our friend, Stu, of *Stampede* however, thinks that it is a very nice thing for them to say. "Why do you think that?" Lois asks. "Well", he explains, "Victor Mike Tango is Naval-ese for VERY MUCH THANK YOU."

The rally is over and all parties attended the fine farewell bash, but no winning trophy for *Que Sera Sera.*

Here at last we quietly settle in for a week to get some rest, and do some serious shopping, for Langkawi is a duty free state and our U.S. dollar is strong against the Malaysian currency.

17

Incredible Thailand

After some relaxation and shopping in the small tourist town of Langkawi, we depart without the fleet, but with our friends on *Sea Gem* and head for Phuket, Thailand. Since we are not going to continue in the Raja Muda Race in Thailand, we are all free to cruise until January 6, 2000, when the rally will leave Thailand for Sri Lanka. Some of the rally crews flew home for the holidays while others enjoyed gunk holing, going from one peaceful anchorage to another, in the Malaysian and Thailand waters.

Our two yachts only go a short distance for we plan to stop at the island of Pulau Dayang Bunting. This is one of the 99 islands that make up the province of Langkawi. On this island we are looking forward to seeing its famous lake, Lake Tasik Dayang Bunting, which means Lake of The Pregnant Maiden. Legend has it a couple was unable to conceive a child for 19 years, yet after drinking from the water the woman became pregnant. It is also said to be home of a white crocodile. One might wonder what part the croc played in the pregnancy.

We walk a short jungle path to the fresh water lake. A dozen monkeys scampering around try to grab our picnic lunch. Not that any of us wants to get pregnant, but we have a swim ourselves. It is a fun, refreshing swim. No white crocodile is spotted, but on the floating swimming platform is a three-foot-long iguana awaiting our return. He is creepy, but does us no harm.

The next day as we head northward, we sail through a large fleet of warships at anchor in the deep water just to the east of Langkawi. Several of the ships are flying the stars and stripes of the U.S.A., but most are from nearby Asian countries, with a few NATO Nations represented as well. It takes us over an hour to sail through the midst of the menacing dark gray ships of war.

Sea Gem hears that there is a fine, modern marina just a few miles along the main island with a resort adjoining it with side-to docks equipped with water and electricity. We make all haste to make the narrow entry at high tide. This marina resort complex is in a man-made hurricane hole and after a call on our VHF radio, we are assigned a dock. We have not been to an actual dock since Singapore; and while electricity is nice to have, fresh water to wash down our salt-stained yachts is most welcome.

Rebak Resort and Marina is privately owned, and it has all the amenities one would expect from a five-star property. A swimming pool, sauna, two restaurants, lounge, and a nice clean laundry room are at our disposal.

Dockage is very inexpensive there, and many transient yachts are tied up at the docks. We meet several of the yachties, and find many have been there since the place opened three years ago. Some of the cruising yachts have so much stuff piled on their decks, that they can not leave the docks without a major reduction in their endless pile of collectibles.

This island paradise is the jumping-off place for those continuing on west across the Indian Ocean to the Red Sea and the Mediterranean or to Africa, and around the Cape of Good Hope. Either way is a big challenge, and so the decision is only made under great stress. Most of these yachts gathered here do not want to decide between the chance of encountering the pirates of the Red Sea or facing the long sea passage to South Africa, and then making it safely past the dangerous Cape of Good Hope.

For us, though, it is only a three-day stop, and off we go to Phuket Island in southernmost Thailand. We didn't get very far because we find what on the charts looks to be a fine protected cove near the Island of Ko Butang. We work our way carefully past several very visible coral heads to pick up a mooring buoy. We are happily attached to the white, sandy bottom, when fellow rally participant, *Pillar G,* also looking to pick up a mooring, finds bottom. Being in eight feet of water, we offer to trade places with them. We do, but find that we too touch bottom so we go to anchor beside *Sea Gem.*

Upon anchoring we find ourselves surrounded by coral. We deploy two anchors to keep from swinging, and then splash overboard to snorkel among the spectacular fish-filled coral. We also celebrate Thanksgiving with a real turkey aboard *Pillar G.*

Off the next day to Phi Phi Don Island. Here we find a large bay on the south side of the island with several yachts already at anchor. The anchorage is fringed with palm trees, and at the far east end of the beach lies a small island strip mall which consists of a couple dozen small wood-framed plastic covered shops selling trinkets, food stalls, and many bars.

We land our dinghies on the beach, and promptly check the place out. As we pull our dinks up the beach, we spot several strange-looking watercraft hauled out there as well. The motor of these crafts is a diesel engine of about 30-horse power with an attached 15-foot long shaft running out behind with a three-bladed propeller. Behind the prop is a small metal scoop also attached to the long tube.

We learn they are called longtails. They look weird, but work very well in the shallow waters surrounding these islands. The engine is mounted on the stern of the boat by a swivel, and so the boat operator can swing the propeller at the end of the shaft and pipe from left to right in an arc of about 250 degrees. When he pushes down on a long handle attached to the front of the engine, the prop will lift clear out of the water, and he can set it back down 90 degrees to his left, and the boat will quickly turn 90 degrees to the left. The little scoop behind the prop will scoop the water up and push it through the tube clear back up to the engine for cooling. We definitely want to have a ride on one of these creatures.

Ride we did the next day as several of us rent a longtail to travel out to Koh Phi Phi Le Island. Our friends, the Grays of *Sea Gem*, Ernst and Christ of *Pimalo* and Brad and Rosie of *Foxy Lady* all join us for a ride. We never tire of boating, so off we go. Koh Phi Phi Le is a high island, but is only a couple of miles in circumference. It has two attractions: the Viking Cave and a spectacular swimming hole carved into a sheer hill.

We tour the Viking Cave named by early European voyagers. It is impressive with numerous signs of past habitation plus several large stalagmites and stalactites.

The highlight of our trip is swimming with the little fishies. There are mooring balls anchored about to protect the coral, so our longtail driver hooks us up to one of them. It is everyone over the side into water about 80 degrees warm. The cove is the habitat of vast schools of sergeant major fish. They engulf us to the extent that I cannot see my mate who is only four feet away.

If they were big, ugly black fish, it would have been frightening, but these are little, blue and yellow-striped fish, about six inches long and are beautiful to see as they slowly parade past my face mask. After snorkeling, we get back in the boat and eat a picnic lunch as we continue to circumnavigate the lush jungle island.

After several days of this pleasant life afloat in paradise, we up our anchor and head northward toward Phuket, stopping at two more anchorages along the way. At the next two island stops we find the waters are greener and greener the further north we travel. Algae is growing here because we are in a large bay on the east side of the island of Phuket where there is less tidal flow and the water temperature is quite high.

The last island anchorage is very green and so full of algae that our water-maker filters plug up. Fish are still plentiful, however, for the bay has several fishnets stretching toward shore. A young native couple come alongside, and offer to sell us some small shrimp. Of course we accept their offer and the fisherman's young wife puts two handfuls of very small shrimp in our bucket. She is quite shy, but smiles at us throughout the bargaining and transfer of the still-alive shrimp.

Phuket Island is about 20 miles long and our marina is at the very northern end of it. When we arrive, we find it to be a new, modern marina with floating side-tie docks, made in Australia. Several of our rally yachts are already there to greet us.

The first full day at the marina, a man comes down the dock asking if anyone needs to have their anchor chain galvanized. We certainly do since it had turned to rust in Port Klang. *Sea Gem* had the same thing happen to its chain; we both dump our chains into a dinghy, and take them to the beach where they are hand-loaded into the back of a pickup truck.

We learn from this businessman that anyone arriving from Malaysia will have a rusty chain and anchors because the tin on the river bottoms eats the galvanized layer away fast. At least five of the yachts arriving with us had to re-galvanize their chains. The cost to totally replate my 275-foot-long chain is 86 U.S. dollars—a very fair price I thought.

After these restoration efforts, we decide to fly to Bangkok, and then to the northern twin cities of Chiang Mai and Chaing Rai at the apex of the Golden Triangle. We make the trip with Charles and Saundra. This is like a visit to another world. It's almost as if Disney had planned the whole area as a fantasy land.

The people are small, all dark-haired, yet light complected, and very beautiful in form and face. They are cheery, fun-loving, and seem to have perpetual smiles on their faces.

We hire a driver-guide for the ten days we are in Chiang Mai. It is a delight to be with Pasith (Peter) Kasuya . He takes us to all of the many tourist sites. We visit more Buddhist temples and orchid gardens. He takes us up the tallest mountain in Thailand overlooking Burma where he lies down in the frost on the side of the trail like a schoolboy. Having never seen snow before, he thinks the frost is snow. A special experience is a visit to an elephant farm where we ride BIG elephants in a narrow river for an hour.

Following his directions, we are led into the foothills of the Himalayas to visit the hill tribe people, who are still living as they did 400 years ago. He hires a longtail to speed us down the Mekong River for a short stop at a native village in Laos. Next we enter the Mae Kok River for a half-day cool, thrilling, and damp ride in a longtail boat to the five-star Dusit Island Resort in Chiang Rai.

The resort is new and luxurious with a fine restaurant on the tenth floor overlooking the river. Here we spend our last evening with Peter, our guide, inviting him to join us for dinner. He declines, out of respect, but eventually yielding to our encouragement, he joins us. Not to be outdone, he gets on stage and with the accompaniment of the band, he sings "My Way" to us. He is very good, and with our eyes closed, he sounds just like Frank Sinatra.

We tour the night market while in Chiang Mai, and buy every rally yacht a small locally-made gift because Christmas is fast approaching. It doesn't seem like Christmas. The trees are all very green and the temperature, even here in the highlands, is usually in the low 70s during the day.

When this fun-filled trip to the hill country is over, we fly back to *Que Sera Sera*. Back at the marina at Phuket, and aboard *Que Sera Sera*, we find that our fleet has split into two groups. Half of the fleet is here and the other half is in another marina closer to the city. Their location is in a more protected harbor than ours, and has a couple of restaurants, one run by an English lady.

Although our little restaurant would normally be closed for Christmas day, our group of sailors convinces her to let us have a Christmas potluck luncheon there. The crews of the yachts attending are *Pimalo, Sea Gem, Prinz Karl, Foxy Lady, Antavina* and *Stampede.* What a fun time we have on this Christmas day!

The fleet cooks present a big delicious meal, followed by a cake made by our host. Although a few other yachties are present, we pretty much have the whole place to ourselves. After the meal, cards are exchanged and Lois presents the brightly wrapped gifts that we purchased in Chiang Mai. Much ado about nothing is made of the unusual gifts, and a fun time is had by all.

The rally organizers arrange to have our combined fleet attend the New Year's Eve celebration at the Cape Panwa Hotel on the very southernmost tip of Phuket. In that it was an hour's drive to get there, we made a reservation to stay overnight. It is a good thing we did for this was one big, wonderful event.

The hotel stands on the top of a small hill overlooking the blue waters of the bay below. The party is held on the beach level under the palm trees, and transportation to the beach is in a small four-person tram. We feel like the king and queen of Thailand as we descend to the beach through the jungle-like setting all around us.

Dinner is served on large tables with white linen tablecloths, fine china, and proper silver settings. This entire splendid array is set up under the gently-rustling palm trees, with the soft lapping of the sea on the sandy shore as accompaniment.

After a fine surf and turf dinner, the celebration begins with local Thai dancers, followed by acrobatics, then an island rock band with four beautiful singers. Fireworks follow and finally a splendid fully decorated huge elephant strides through our midst.

What a fabulous place to bring in the New Year with our new sailing comrades. What a spectacular night it is—the dawn of the new century— the millennium celebration!

Even though there are fireworks bursting in the air, lots of hugs and kissing at midnight, I keep one eye on the lights of the resort high on the hill above us to see if they go out. None of us quite know what is going to happen as a result of the Y2K phenomenon when computers change to the new century.

Son Fred had asked me to give him a call if they do go out, for that would give him eight hours' warning that all hell is about to befall the U.S. of A. I don't know what he expected to do with the warning, but knowing Fred, he would have made good use of the extra eight hours.

This small country has been an exceptional place. Every day was totally different. We will never forget the unusual things we saw, and the beautiful, gentle people who made for a great time. It was the most exciting country we had been in, and we loath the idea of pulling up anchor and moving on.

18

Sri Lanka Saga

Next we visit the storied island nation of Sri Lanka. It is well known to sailors as a safe and hospitable place to stop, rest, and gather provisions for the arduous trip to the Red Sea. After having been there, we would have to say that someone has been stretching the truth just a little.

We are anchored in a half moon-shaped bay about a mile and a half wide and a mile deep, but totally open to the south in Galle. Normally that shouldn't make any difference because the wind predominately comes from the northeast, but as winds will do, they come from the wrong direction at the wrong time.

So the second day here, the winds doth blow from the southwest and they blow hard. We tuck up under the point that sticks out from the southwest so we don't get the full seas in our face, but the sea swells still roll around. Other boats anchored further to the east have a bad time, and one even drags far enough toward the beach that rally people have to board and move it out of harm's way.

We are concerned that we might drag as well, but the next day when we try to up anchor, the chain is wrapped around a big rock so we should not have worried at all. That causes us to miss our scheduled fueling time in the inner harbor because we have to ask our friend Ern from the yacht *Pimalo* to dive and set our anchor free.

We have one other little incident though which was the loss of a dinghy after the big blow. Not our dinghy, of course, for our dinghy is tied up in its bag on deck safe and sound. It is *Prinz Karl*'s that we are keeping watch over while he tours, that somehow drifts away during the night off the stern of our boat. Not to worry though, for being a good friend, I set off to find his lost dinghy. After hunting in all the logical places with no luck, good old me goes to the harbor police to report that it has gone missing. Lots of pirates and dangerous Tamal Tiger terrorists around, they say.

I'm introduced to Officer Shelton of the harbor police and he says, "Let's go look for it." Now the police don't have a vehicle free to look for a dinghy, so I must hire a three-wheeled tuk tuk vehicle to do the searching. Finally way out on the northwest end of the bay, we arrive at the lighthouse, and lo and behold, the guys that are painting the lighthouse announce that they found the dinghy at 6:30 in the morning. They bring it ashore with no harm done to it. It was already deflated and stored with an engine on top of the second floor of the storage building. They are happy to turn it over to Officer Shelton and me. Perhaps they had heard that I was offering a 5000 rupee reward for returning my good friend's dinghy (5000 rupees = 70 U.S.).

So I pay the 5000 rupees to the lighthouse painters. The tuk tuk driver gets a big wad of rupees for driving us around for two hours, and hauling the dinghy back on top of his tuk tuk. With those guys well taken care of, I slip my now good friend, Officer Shelton, the last money in my wallet— a 100 U.S. dollar bill.

Talk about a big smile, Officer Shelton almost rips his face in half when he sees the big green bill in my hand. I pump the dinghy back up and proceed to take it back out and double tie it on the stern of the owner's boat this time instead of mine.

Here the plot thickens. When riding around on the lost dinghy search, Officer Shelton just happens to mention that he suffered an injury to his hip when he was younger, and he needs an operation to get it fixed. He says that he has an appointment next month to have it operated on, and that he only needs $700 U.S. more for the operation. He even pulls out a medical form to show me the doctor's report.

I guess the $100 is not enough help because he invites Lois and me to his house to meet his family. We accept and three days later we go to lunch at his house.

We meet his wife, his daughter, his son, and his father. Also in attendance are his two brothers, his well-educated sister-in-law, and most memorable of all is his wee grandmother. We enjoy lunch until he asks for another large money donation on the way back to the boat.

Sri Lanka is currently involved in a small civil war in the north which affects the southern region of Galle where we are bobbing around at anchor because the Sri Lanka Navy has a small base here. Obviously they want to protect their WW II sub chaser and a couple of equally old small escort vessels. These vessels are located in the inner basin where yachties usually are permitted to tie up, but our millennium fleet is not allowed to do so for some reason. That was good, for the inner basin usually has a layer of diesel fuel covering the whole area. That basin is indeed where we have to go through the entry procedure .

The rally has an agreement with customs and immigration that our fleet will all clear at once instead of one at a time which would have required at least three stops: port authority, customs, and immigration, all at different locations.

So we proceed to the dinghy dock inside the inner harbor and lo and behold there are all three officialdoms at portable tables to check us in. This is great except for the oil that is now all over our newly launched dinghy's clean bottom and hull sides. This harbor is so bad that somebody's or something's lower intestines are seen floating around the dinghy dock.

We complete the normal checking-in routine and all gather at the old English Victorian hotel overlooking the eastern end of the bay. Five of our fleet are at anchor below the verandah. The view is splendid as we gaze over the coconut palms to the Indian Ocean beyond.

About 2300 hrs. we all pile into our various dinghies, and head back to our respective vessels to turn in for the night, but when we get to the inner harbor exit we are stopped by a Navy patrol launch carrying three men bearing arms.

They are friendly though, and just ask a few general questions. "Do you have any weapons?" NO," we quickly answer. "Do you have any ammunition?" "NO!" "You may proceed." You bet we proceed.

The next morning, as we enter the inner oil-slick-coated harbor, we notice on each end of the breakwall there is a black box structure with four windows. There are several uniformed men with AK 47 or KA 74's standing in the open windows. We just wave, smile, say hi, and hope they are in a friendly mood.

This goes on for several days and nights. Each dinghy must stop and answer questions about arms. They riffle through our bags and then send us on out around the big rope they have strung across the harbor entrance.

After a week of this, we're starting to get used to it. But then one night we return from dinner to a different scene. Spotlights shine in our faces from the guardhouse. The patrol boat approaches, we stop, they search, they ask questions. We say we don't have weapons, they say OK. But wait one guy has a stick in his hand—a stick with a tail.

"Hey! What's that in your hand there?" "This," he says as he lifts it up so all aboard our fragile, rubber inflatable dinghy can see. "Its DYNAMITE!!!!"

Ssssshhhiiiit. "What's that for?" we ask. "To discourage scuba divers from entering the harbor," he says. "Ya want ta see?" He lights the fuse, sparks fly, hearts thump, and as we start to move away he throws the stick into the oil-coated water. The water jumps a couple of feet high in the air, and we hear a big "kerthump". We leave the next day for India not knowing that three weeks later we would hear even more of the lost dinghy saga.

While in the northern Maldives waiting to get our cruising permit from customs, we are talking to a fellow sailor who has just arrived from Sri Lanka. When we mention that it was not our favorite stop, he launches into a mild foaming-at-the-mouth narration of his experience while in Galle, Sri Lanka with the harbor police.

Our fellow sailor recounts his story: "Having arrived after a rough seven-day-passage from Phuket, Thailand to Galle, my crew and I proceed into the inner, oil-coated harbor, tie up our dinghy, and walk to the scenic hotel on the hill to contemplate our successful crossing, and of course down a few beers.

After drinking whatever the hotel has to offer in the way of spirits, we amble back to the dinghy dock. Much to our surprise no dinghy is to be found at either the dock or anywhere else in the harbor. Having no luck in a short search, we go to the harbor police.

So it turns out none of the on-duty officers know anything about our missing dinghy, but seeing as we cannot return to our boat without a dinghy, we are given wooden benches to sleep on in the hall of the police station. The benches were in a hallway open on two sides, one of which faced the mosquito-infested courtyard. We have no blankets to hide under. Between the mosquitoes and the very cool night air, we suffer more than we sleep.

The next morning the police report they found our dinghy earlier when the day shift came on duty. Where is it now, I ask?

"It's right over there around the corner of the police station. Yeah really, it was there all night. One of the officers found it after dark and brought it here," is his response.

My sailor friend says, "Yeah! Sure one of their officers found it, my ass. They stole the damn thing and they wanted a reward. They said the last guy that lost his dinghy offered a $75 US dollar reward and didn't I think my dinghy was worth a reward?"

"Oh! Oh!" Quietly I say to him, "I might have created a monster." He says, "What do you mean by that? Are you the guy that gave the bastards the reward? You better believe you created a monster. I was the fourth one since you forked over the cash for your dinghy. They have a real scam going on there."

The big, troubled sailor scowls when I ask if it was Officer Shelton who asked for the reward. His reply was, "Nah, I know that guy. I don't think he was there."

That answer should make my conscience clear, but for some reason I still feel a little guilty. Does anyone want to help Officer Shelton pay for his hip operation? Or better yet help pay off his property? I have his direct bank deposit number.

19

Trading Dollars for Foreign Currency

The rally organizers have planned a brief stop in Cochin, India on our way to the Maldives. *Que Sera Sera* is the first to arrive, and so we have to blaze the way.

Cochin is not a normal cruising stop; it has no local sailors nor docks. We anchor in a shallow area at the split of the two main shipping channels which is directly in front of a five-star hotel. The hotel has a dock, but it is small and off limits to check into customs and immigration.

That issue is solved when around the corner of the channel comes a large rowboat, rowed in tandem by two young Indian men. They promptly head directly toward us, and come alongside of our boat. All smiles, they welcome us to Cochin in very understandable English. The lead man states that we should not launch our dinghy with a motor because it will be stolen, and that they will take us to shore or to old Cochin City.

We get to know the two young boatmen quite well as they ferry us from our anchorage three or four times a day. In fact, one of the men, Nazar, invites us to his home to meet his entire family. What an interesting invitation that turns out to be.

He picks us up in his rowboat after his daily rowing is complete, and it is getting rather dark when we arrive at the boat docks in Old Cochin. He leads us off the narrow, wooden dock, and into a narrow alleyway to some old, seemingly empty warehouses. Lois is following him closely, and I am walking a couple of paces behind her. Just as Lois gets off the dock, I noticed movement close behind her down at the water. Rats—lots of them. I didn't make a peep for if she saw those loathsome critters, all hell would break loose. Lois doesn't care for the long, black-tailed beady-eyed monsters. We have just barely gotten ashore, and things are already getting a little hairy.

We proceed on down the alley past the dark warehouses onto one of Old Cochin's many, narrow streets. There are street lights along the way, but very few and far between so the street is dimly lit with strange shadows casting unusual shapes around us.

There are few men around as we walk down the now quiet street for a few blocks. We stop under one of the street lights where women are gathered, filling metal containers with water that is spewing forth from something similar to a fire hydrant. Their chattering stops as we approach and dozens of faces turn our way to stare at two tall, light-skinned foreigners. Nazar greets his sister who is among them.

We are then led down a long, low-roofed hallway with small rooms on both sides to the fifth room on the left, which is their home. As we enter by way of a cloth drape, he introduces us to his wife, who is nursing her new baby as she sits on the dirt floor, and his mother and three school-aged children. He asks us to have a seat on the wooden bench just inside the doorway.

If we stretched our arms out, we could almost touch the wall across the room; that's how small the room is. We think this must be Nazar's and his wife's room, and that his mother and father sleep on the wooden bench we are sitting on and that their son sleeps on the floor next to them. There is a single bare light bulb hanging in the middle of the ceiling.

As Nazar's mother offers us coffee or tea, I receive a questioning look from my love wondering if drinking the water will be safe. After a moment realizing that turning down their offer would probably be offensive to these kind people, and that the tea will be boiled and thus not likely to do harm to our delicate digestive tracks, I say, "Tea, please."

We drink our tea, and after a delightful conversation during which no one asks for money, Nazar takes us back to our equally small house afloat in the bay.

Nazar and his younger friend, Naheeb, manually row a 20-foot wooden boat back and forth from the commercial docks to the port city of old Cochin many times a day for 1800 rupees a trip, or about $3 U.S. They are allowed to carry up to 19 people per trip across the channel, and the trip takes them 15 minutes each way. It sounds like they could make some good money, but there are at least six other boats vying for the same few people, and the boats belong to someone else.

Later I explain that I have to get ashore to check in with officialdom. Nazar says that he will take me to shore and lead me to the proper authorities. Leaving Lois aboard by herself, I climb in and they row me in, and quickly lead me to the port captain's office. This checking-in process itself becomes a half-day of standing around and practicing patience. First I tackle the port control authorities, next customs, and then the longest and furthest away, immigration.

The big problem is that usually only one person in the three government offices that I have to visit speaks English. If that person is busy or out of the office , I wait patiently. I left our boat just after 1 in the afternoon and arrive back to my waiting, worrying mate just a little after 4 p.m. with some interesting tales to share.

With all of our many trips to shore to clear customs, immigration and harbor police from our anchorage, plus to the restaurant several times, we surely augmented the boat boy's wages considerably.

Our boat friends find a tuk tuk driver to take us to the Internet café to gather, and send our e-mail. They guide us to the old historic sights of the formerly Portuguese, Dutch, and then British-occupied city. We even visit the Old Christian Church of 1503 that once held Vasco da Gama's remains.

Old Cochin was just that, old. Settled first by the Portuguese in 1500, the city is laid out similarly to any city in Portugal—narrow streets, open sewer drains along the streets, with housing crowded right on the edge of the street. That may have been all right in Europe before the age of cars and buses, but now throw in beeping tuk tuks, goats by the dozens, an occasional sacred cow, and then stir in a few hundred people all trying to get down the street at the same time, and you can imagine the utter chaos that overwhelms this crowded city. Add to that mayhem, the dirty smells wafting up from the open, foul sewer drains, and in amongst all this are street vendors selling all kinds of little trinkets, clothes, aluminum pots and pans, plus the fruit and vegetable stands on every corner.

The modern city of Ernakuiam across the river from Old Cochin, however, is different. Over-crowded buses, more tuk tuks, more people, many times more cars, but no cows or goats, and with slightly wider streets. The streets are full of potholes, and under constant repair by people using hand tools. The putrid sewers are still along the roadside, but at least they are mostly covered.

In Cochin begging is outlawed, and the law is respected. We had seen some very grotesque and large scale begging in Sri Lanka where children were maimed to beg for their families.

St. Thomas, the disciple, known as doubting Thomas, is believed to have been in this area in 59 AD, so there are many Christian churches to visit rather than the Buddhist temples that we had been visiting in Thailand and Malaysia. Because the English spent sufficient time in India, the schools teach English so that most of the young people and business people speak pretty good English. It makes getting around very easy. We chose not to go north into the big cities of Bombay and Calcutta, but rather stay close to our floating home.

We have an interesting and somewhat trying experience the next morning after we realize we don't have any rupees to spend during a visit to Old Cochin. The rowboat taxi driver returns and, realizing our situation, offers to lead me to the bank on the same street where the hotel is located.

"Let's do that," I reply. Off I go with my wallet in pocket, once again leaving my mate to guard our little ship. Once back to the rowboat dock, I walk ashore, and my rowboat guide calls over to a three-wheeled motor bike and directs the driver to take me to the bank, about two miles down the road.

We pull up in front of the National Bank of India, a huge one story building close to 100 yards long from end to end. Upon entering the main entrance, I pass by two bank guards, who seem not to notice the westerner entering the bank.

Now in the lobby, I look to the right and then to the left searching for someone to talk to about getting a few rupees. In front of me is a counter running the entire length of the bank, but there is no receptionist or clerk in sight.

I finally spot three men a short way to my left, closer to the counter, so I head toward them. I stand directly in front of the first one I come to, but he never looks up. Even when I speak to him he doesn't look up. So I move to the next man, and hold up my credit card. He glances at me, then at the credit card, and then his head starts to swivel. His head swivels smoothly from left to right, and then right to left, all the while sort of nodding up and down. He then turns to the man next to him, and that guy's head begins to swivel as well. This swiveling head action sure got a big smile out of me, but still no action out of them. Finally the furthest man to the left gets up approaches me, and in very ragged English says, "No! We cannot help you." After having already spent almost seven U.S. dollars to get there, and an hour of my time, I ask to see the manager of the bank. The swivel head points to the office to my left.

The door to the office is open so I waltz right in to speak to the manager. The receptionist just around the corner appears, and asks me to please sit down. I sit for several minutes checking the place out carefully. The room, except for the young girl's desk and chair, is barren. Cheap fake wood wallboard walls, no pictures, no plaques proclaiming excellence or banking honors, not even a picture of the king, well, prime minister. The name on a small metal plate on the office door says president. The president is going to personally see me. Be patient, Don.

In the office of the president, I am greeted by a smart-looking younger man dressed in a blue suit and tie. He bid me sit down and asks how he can help me. I hold up my credit card, he takes it and studies it, and then asks for my passport. I have never needed my passport to get cash from my Visa card before so I had not brought it with me. He shakes his head and makes a call on his phone. A few minutes later my friend, the swivel head, appears in the door. The president holds up my Visa card in front of the man, and his head begins to swivel again. I'm wondering if my Visa card holds some amazing power over this guy's head. With this silent signal the president turns back to me and says, "No, we can not give you any rupees."

Well, I have to get some rupees, so I ask him if he could change a 100 dollar bill. He looks back at the clerk and repeats my question in Indian. With only a little head movement he says, "Yes, but I still must see your passport."

With a patient thank you, I bid them goodbye, and I walk back the two miles to the dinghy dock. I only had to wait about twenty minutes for my boat taxi to cross the river, and pick me up to take me back to the boat, and my ever-waiting mate.

It is well past noon, so Lois makes us lunch, and with passport in hand off we row back to the taxi dock. From there I hop onto the three-wheeled tuk tuk taxi, and head back to the bank.

In I go, again past the two guards into the main hall, and head directly to the last swivel head behind the long counter. He sees me coming, I know, but even when I stop directly in front of his position, he continues to ignore me. Patiently I hold up my United States of America 100 dollar bill and my passport. After a long pause he nods in my general direction, gets up from his desk, and heads over to the president's office.

Soon he returns, and asks for my passport and the $100 bill. In exchange he hands me a large gold coin, gold in color only, with the number 43 on it, and points me toward the right end of the hallway.

As I get close to the far right end I see three chicken wire- enclosed cages with small square openings facing the hall. Behind one of the openings sits a man, a teller I hope. Over the first cage is a box with red lighted numbers on it. The flashing number is 22. I look again at my gold coin with the number 43 and sit down to wait. Wait for whom? There were no other people sitting on the row of old wooden chairs beside me.

The numbers begin to click down quickly until they reach 31, and then they stop. Not 30 seconds after this stoppage, in walks a large man. He is wearing the bank's light-blue uniform and is carrying a double-barreled shot gun. He walks five paces past me, and sits down on a chair at the very end of the hall. He seems to have a pleasant persona, but his weapon is very menacing, so I only glance his way a couple of times, and then sit quietly feeling very small.

The number is now up to 40. Progress for sure, but the clicking numbers soon stop, and the teller leaves his chicken coop. Not long after his departure guards enter the bank carrying a big wooden trunk that looks to be quite heavy. They lug it through an opening in the long counter, and then into the cage the teller has just left.

Shortly they leave, and I wait longingly. It is as if time is standing still, and the number is frozen at 40. Only the shot gun moves occasionally on the guard's lap. Is he here to protect me or the bank?

I run out of patience! With a short backward glance toward the double-barreled enforcer, I head back to my favorite swivel head and hold up my gold coin with number 43 stamped on it. It works just like my Visa card, his head swivels several times, and then he gets up and smiles at me. I didn't smile back at him, I fear. I state clearly that he has my 100 dollars and my passport, and I have no rupees.

He asks for my gold coin. How dumb am I, I give it to him? He quickly walks off toward the back of the great hall to yet another seated man along the back wall. Now he has my passport, my 100 dollar bill, and my gold coin. Not long though he comes back, hands me my coin, and points back to the cages, and the shot gun.

Click number 43 at last, and in a nanosecond I am standing in front of the chicken wire. The teller is lifting big stacks of money out of the treasure chest. Each bundle is close to an inch thick, and is held together by a huge industrial-strength staple. He is using a screwdriver to remove the staple.

After removing the staple from five bundles, he counts out bills and then pushes them along with my passport through the little opening in the wire. I don't know how many rupees I have, but I get the better part of five bundles for one, thin U.S. one hundred dollar bill. I was grinning!

I even grin at the shotgun-bearing guard, who is now protecting me from being robbed of all of my piles of rupees. My patience has finally paid off big time, for now I'm a rupee millionaire.

As I depart the bank and step once again outside, almost three hours later, I glance up and down the street expecting Butch Cassidy and the Sundance Kid to come galloping into town, not to rob me of course, but rather the blue, uniformed bankers of Cochin.

20

MALDIVES, A PLACE OF BEAUTY

We didn't mind leaving Cochin, and have a good sail south to the Maldives. En route we catch a nice, fat tuna, which is always a delightful change in menu. The last morning out we have some heavy rain and wind, which is the first in a very long time.

Upon arriving at the first most northern atoll in the Maldives, we anchor off the small village of Toulican. We are visited by the officials, and told that we can check in at 5 p.m. We have a leisurely afternoon aboard, and then launch our dinghy to go ashore. After a walk in the spotlessly clean village, we find the customs man, but he is in the midst of a heated volleyball game, and kindly suggests that we come back the next day. We didn't think about the fact that we are now in a Muslim country, and that Friday is their holy day.

We stay three nights at the island, where we see two big sea turtles, and several manta rays with at least ten-foot wingspans. One of us, being a little brave, gets in and swims with three of them. The other not so brave crewman plays lifeguard from the boat.

The next day we are issued a cruising permit to allow us to travel south through the island chain to the capital city, Male', three days south. Our permit states that we are only to stop at resort islands, and we are not allowed on islands where the locals live. So it was a real treat to visit with the locals, and to see the way they live here on this most northern, tourist island.

They use U.S .currency, and even 160 miles north of Male', they don't want to give us Maldivian money for U.S. dollars. They can change $100 U.S. into smaller US bills at the grocery store. The wide-eyed children all flock around to stare at our pale faces, and those 10 years or older come to practice their English .

The thing that amazes us is the cleanliness. All roads are hard-packed sand, and bikes are the only means of transportation. We see no garbage or loose trash as we did in India and Sri Lanka. The government buildings are all new plastered concrete blocks, thoroughly white-washed with ceramic tile floors. Everyone is dressed nicely, the men in western clothes, and the women in saris of beautiful colors. We are told that bathing suits are not permitted on the beach, and not to invite locals aboard our boat.

These Maldives are truly a magical place in the Indian Ocean. Crystal clear waters glisten in the sun around these islands, scattered along a north-south line 470 miles long crossing the equator.

Each island has its own coral barrier reef to both protect it from the ocean surf, and to delight the snorkeler and scuba divers alike with underwater sights. The government has outlawed fishing with any type of nets or spear guns so the water literally swarms with every kind of fish of all shapes and colors.

The barrier reefs do limit where a yacht might anchor safely without going bump in the night on a big bombie. A bombie is a very large, hard coral head growing up from the bottom. When the tide changes, the boat may float over one of them and make contact. We find a coral-free strip of white sand where we drop our anchor. We think it is a good solution, until the next morning when the resort seaplane comes blasting wingtip-close to our rigging as it takes off. It seems we have anchored on top of the seaplane runway. After the second one comes roaring by, we up anchor and move over a few hundred yards. We couldn't see the runway in the water.

After sailing 45 miles further south the next day, we drop anchor about 100 yards off a local village just before dark. Our cruising permit did not allow us to visit native island villages, but it seems OK to just stay aboard.

As darkness falls a small, wooden boat rows out to us, with a schoolteacher, the chief's son, the assistant chief's son, and a fisherman. We talk for a long time, and then we invite them aboard one at a time to see our home. They are very polite, curious, and talk with us for a couple of hours. As a reward for our friendship and hospitality, the next day the fisherman brings us his first catch—a nice tuna.

Just as we are getting ready to leave, we notice that all the women from the village are frantically sweeping the beach with palm fronds. When they see that we are not coming ashore they slowly return back up the now clean beach to their homes amongst the palm trees, obviously disappointed. We wish we had gone ashore, for they must have been preparing a welcoming for us.

The next 40 miles takes us to a resort island with bungalows, seaplanes, restaurants, and at last, a phone to call home. When we call my parents to check on my mother and say happy birthday to my Dad, for six minutes our bill was $78 US.

We motor all the next day to a small resort island on yet another big 15 x 10 mile atoll, arriving a couple of hours before sunset. We cruise along close to shore just outside the coral that fringes the beach. On the port side of the boat in the crystal clear water, we can see the coral, and on the starboard side is only blue water, over 100 feet deep. Undaunted we move to the next island three miles south.

This island seems to have a little shelf between the deep and the coral, so we drop the big anchor with chain and a trip line with a float in the deep water, and back in close to the reef. I jump into the dinghy with the stern anchor, find a sandy spot, drop the anchor fast, and return to take up the line on the bow anchor.

My mate keeps the engine in slow forward, pulling on the stern anchor to hold us off while I take up on the forward anchor even more. We soon realize that the fore anchor is now straight down the wall into the 100 plus feet of dark, deep water. The rudder is about six feet from a couple of bombies, one on either side, and as soon as we put the engine in neutral we slide sideways in the current and bounce the rudder on one or both.

I jump back in the dinghy, and quickly run out a third anchor off the middle of the starboard side to hold us against the current. We bump the bombies a couple of times hard with the rudder again, but it looks like we can stay.

Just to be sure I don my snorkel gear, and go in the water to check my three anchors. The bow anchor is indeed going straight down a vertical cliff wall out of sight, and so is my 50-foot long trip float that is attached to it. The side anchor is caught behind a medium-sized chunk of dead coral only two feet from the cliff face. It seems that if the boat swings the other way, it will go over the top of it, and into the deep water as well. So I swim over to inspect the stern anchor that had held us so well. The Danforth is standing on its side caught not in sand, but behind a very small piece of dead coral and looks like one big tug will pull it free.

Large areas of coral, in all the northern Maldives were killed off during an El Nino year due to increased water temperature. Sadly not very colorful coral, but there are a lot of beautiful fish swimming around, checking my anchors with me.

So, with the sun about to plunge into the sea and us into darkness, we pull up all the iron pieces we had spread around and head out into deep waters outside the atoll. With no other seemingly good places to anchor, we choose to head further south. We motor all night to Male', and are rewarded in the morning by the sight of several of the masts of our fellow rally boats who, having skipped India, are already at anchor. We anchor in a beautiful lagoon inside the reef of the island of Furanafushi which is on the east side of the large North Male' Atoll. Here we find white sandy beaches all fringed with palm trees, and an occasional bathing suit-clad tourist.

The Maldives are made up of 1192 small islands. This is one of 74 special islands set aside for resorts only. We have dinner ashore with our friends, the Grays of *Sea Gem,* at a very modern classy Italian restaurant.

In Male' itself we are told we can find a cyber net café, phones, lettuce, and all the good things big bucks will buy. Nothing is grown or manufactured in the islands, but you can get anything you want for a price. It's good news though, since we will be traveling over 2000 miles to Djibouti, and our ship's provisions are low since Sri Lanka and India were not very good places to stock up.

The islands are inhabited by tribes believed to have come from India and Sri Lanka, but the Portuguese arrived aboard merchant sailing ships sailing eastward. Male' was the center of their early colonization. They weren't here too long before the Dutch arrived and took possession of the many islands. Next the English Navy commenced to throw the Dutch out.

The Brits departed in 1968, and since then European tourists have invaded the islands in ever growing numbers. The local Muslim island residents are not allowed to visit or work on the 74 designated tourist-only islands. The workers come from India and Sri Lanka, and are not allowed to visit any island not designated as a tourist island.

Before our departure the crews have a wonderful Valentine's Day celebration on the island of Kurumba. The resort sends a guest motor launch out to the anchorage, and takes us to the resort main dock. As the sun is setting, we are guided past the elegant lanai cabins, through the richly landscaped grounds to the beach where we are all seated at a long table. Palm trees rustle over our heads, and the water laps gently on the sandy beach just a few feet behind us. An elegant buffet dinner is laid out under the gently swaying date palm trees, and all the while a live band plays along with the soft song of the sea.

We will be traveling in convoys due to the pirate-infested areas of Yemen and Somalia that we will soon be sailing through. There will be five boats in our group, three American boats, plus our Tahitian friends, and Ernst and Chris of the yacht *Pimalo,* our new friends from Luxembourg. The French Navy has given us a way point which all of us must cross at which time we will turn our single side band radios on to their frequency, and report to confirm our location. Then we will stop using our VHF radios unless we have an emergency.

The Maldives islands may not quite be paradise, but one could certainly spend an eternity here and be very happy, for it is indeed a beautiful place on this vast ocean.

21

A Very Unusual Crossing

We have done several long distance ocean crossings, but this one will stand out as the most unusual. All 17 vessels of the rally will make the long voyage to Djibouti, Africa— a little over 2,000 nautical miles west. This would be our longest non-stop leg since Chile to the Tuamotu Islands.

We stagger our starting times to allow the boats traveling at the same speed to be able to stay within VHF range of each other for the entire passage. Being the smallest, we start at about 10 o'clock in the morning. *Pimalo* (42 ft.) and *Prinz Karl* (53 ft.) start shortly thereafter, for though they may be a little faster, they have agreed to sail together with us.

Several hours later *Sea Gem* (54 ft.) departs Male' to meet us. Then follow the fast boats, the catamaran *Antaviana* (47 ft.), *Pilar G* (66 ft.), and *Die Swaene* (90 ft.) catching up quickly. These four big yachts blew by us some time the first night out of port.

The 58-foot yacht, *Stampede,* with Stu and July Conway aboard was to have started with us, but due to a crewman's injury they will start the next day. The crewman, Joey, had fallen out of his fast-moving inflatable dinghy and had been hit in the face by the spinning propeller of the engine as it came back around to him. Luckily another rally member saw him, and realized that he could not get back in the still-circling craft. Patrick, the skipper of *Allegra B,* quickly jumped in his dinghy and fished out the badly bleeding young man before the many sharks sensed his blood in the water, or worse yet, he passed out from shock.

Due to the varying speeds of the boats, within the first two or three days the fleet is scattered all over the ocean. The only contact with each other is by SSB radio.

On the second day we are only three boats sailing to windward wondering what has become of our great plan to stick together. That's OK because we three are all good friends, good sailors, and have cruised together before. Early the third day, lo and behold *Sea Gem* appears somehow just a couple miles ahead of us. So now we are four.

Sea Gem's skipper, Charlie, has been in communication with Stu of *Stampede* on SSB, and he informs us that Stu is trying to catch up with us. He has to motor at less than five knots due to a leak in his prop shaft seal, and asks if we could slow down for him.

We four, having no wind at the time and wishing to accommodate our fellow sailor, magnanimously stop our vessels at sunset and wait all night on a glassy smooth sea for them.

By 0900 the next morning we get a call on the VHF radio, "Any Millennium Odyssey yacht, this is the sailing vessel *Stampede* calling." They are about 15 miles astern so we crank up our engines and slowly head off for distant Djibouti. Now there are five.

The winds fill in again, but unfortunately from the nor-nor-west, and we want to sail northwest. The sea begins to build with wind, and we have a wet beat to windward. This adverse wind lasts for 36 hours, and then is followed by a night of no winds. Motors come on, and we all chug along rolling to and fro in the leftover seas.

After about 24 hours of motoring, we all start to consider how we will ever make it the remaining 1,200 miles motoring for only *Sea Gem* has enough fuel to motor that far. We start looking for alternate ports within range of our fast depleting fuel.

There's a small port in southern Oman that the ocean guide book says has a place we can fill jerry cans from the local fuel station. Lugging jerry cans a half a mile is not what we'd like to be doing, but fuel is fuel, and we need a lot of it, and we've never been to Oman before. So we all set our courses for Shalala, Oman, in our GPSs and off we go again.

We didn't have to motor long for the wind fills back in, but still from the nor-nor west, luckily not as strong as the previous day. We ride that fair wind for two days until the wind starts to clock around more to the north for a day, and then it goes east for us at last.

Now six days out of a port, even two yachts would normally be separated from each other by several miles, but since *Stampede* arrived we have never, day or night, been out of sight of each other. Sometimes it may be hard for the lead boat to see the last boat, but usually with good sun or a pair of binoculars they can be spotted.

On the seventh day the crew of *Prinz Karl* announces on VHF that they have caught a 110-pound yellow fin tuna, and ask if anyone wants some fresh fish for dinner. Sure comes the reply from *Pimalo* and from *Que Sera Sera.* As darkness is falling, and as a big ship is passing the fleet, Teva brings his yacht up to our stern, and passes us a bag full of fresh cleaned tuna and a chilled bottle of wine. I'm sure the passing ship must have wondered why three small sailboats were milling around in circles as the sun set in the middle of the Arabian Sea.

Each day now the wind continues to clock further to the east, and the breeze holds at 12 to 14 knots, so broad-reaching to Oman is the order of the day. *Sea Gem* and *Pimalo* are so close one day that they spent an hour taking pictures of each other's boats under full sail.

On the sixth day out, we receive a call on SSB from one of the rally yachts that had started from Cochin, India that they would like to rendezvous with our fleet. Charlie of *Sea Gem*, our fleet navigator, gives him a GPS coordinate on our rhumb line, a straight line from one point to another, to Oman, and says we'll meet you there in two days. So sure enough two days hence our sixth fleet member, the yacht *Santana*, finds us at that tiny spot on the sea.

On we sail now toward Oman, checking off our once-distant way points as we pass them. Now we have six boat lights to keep track of in the night. Luckily a full moon certainly helps that problem.

One night *Stampede* was so close behind us that when the moon arose in the eastern sky their masthead light was weaving slowly back and fourth across the moon's bright orange face. It only lasts a few minutes, but is definitely an unusual sight to see.

The next day *Prinz Karl's* crew catch two more yellow fin tunas, but they are much smaller than the giant of two days before. Once again they made the rounds handing out fish from the fish market yacht.

We have our asymmetrical spinnaker up most of the day, and *Pimalo* has their spinnaker set and flying nicely. We just happened to be close enough to each other after a few hours that we converge for some extensive picture taking of each other's boats while steaming at six knots along under full sail.

The morning of the twelfth day, and after a near miss night collision between *Prinz Karl* and *Que Sera Sera*, the boats still remain within visual distance of each other.

The weather is fine with warm, sunny days and nice, cool sweater-weather nights for the watch keeper. With steady winds of 12 to 14 abaft the beam to keep our boats moving westward, now we can head directly to Djibouti instead of being diverted to Oman.

This day is also a spinnaker-flying day, which is good for little *Que Sera Sera*. Today for about an hour, we sail within 30 feet of *Pimalo* on one side, and *Prinz Karl* on the other side. *Sea Gem* is only a few dozen yards ahead with his spinnaker full and pulling as well.

We are soon to find out that this close quarter fleet sailing might be a little risky. Just before dark *Sea Gem*, out a half mile in front of *Pimalo*, drops its spinnaker which reduces its speed slowly from six knots to five. Now it happens that all on *Pimalo* have gone below for dinner, so they don't notice *Sea Gem's* reduction in sail and corresponding reduction in speed.

All aboard *Sea Gem* also go below for just a few minutes, and get involved in other diversionary chores, and do not realize that *Pimalo* is still sailing at six knots until there is a loud smash against their hull. Not just one, but three, for it took *Pimalo's* captain a few seconds to dash up to the cockpit to disengage the auto pilot and steer away.

The loud smashing sounds must have annoyed the great wind maker in the sky for soon he shut off our abaft of the beam winds, and we all motor through the night.

The next day brought a clear sunny sky. We motor on until we get a call that *Santana* needs to slow down because its engine is over-heating. On the radio much information on what could be causing this problem is offered by the captains. When *Santana* ran fewer than five knots, his engine ran cool, the skipper reports, so we all slow to five knots.

On *Que Sera Sera,* fearing that our fuel will not last until Djibouti, we contact our fleet fuel tanker, *Sea Gem,* to see if they can offload a couple of jerry jugs to us. "Sure" they say, "Come on over."

We promptly tie four, five-gallon plastic jerry cans on the end of a 100-foot line, and drop them in the water while motoring along just in front of *Sea Gem*. They quickly fish them aboard with the boat hook, and we head back on course for Djibouti.

As we look back a short while later we see *Prinz Karl* looking very tiny on the eastern horizon, and so promptly gave them a call on VHF radio.

"What's wrong, *Prinz Karl*?" "Oh, nothing; the autopilot quit working and Teva has it apart all over the cockpit, but he almost has it fixed. Don't worry," says the little first mate, Hinano.

On to Djibouti we go, but soon *Santana* is dropping back from the fleet again. Another VHF call to Matt on *Santana* finds that his engine is now overheating at anything over three knots. Now we do have a big problem for we all must maintain at least five knots to be able to get to Djibouti in time for the crews of three of the boats, who are either flying out or flying in, to meet them.

Now what do we do? Well, it happens that a few days back we all had thought that we might have to go to Al Mukalla, Yemen for fuel, so we had a position marked in our GPSs, and that destination is 76 miles to the northeast.

The decision is made that since we all can't make Djibouti, *Que Sera Sera* will take *Santana* in tow and head for Al Mukalla. *Stampede* very emphatically tells us that we are not going without them so they will follow us. Within a half-hour after making this decision, *Que Sera Sera* has *Santana* in tow and the three yachts are headed off to visit Yemen with the other three yachts continuing on to Djibouti.

The tow goes well through the dark night until about 4 a.m. when we encounter a westbound ship fast approaching on our course. *Stampede* calls it on VHF channel sixteen with no response, *Que Sera* calls as well, but no reply is forthcoming, and our position is looking problematic. With *Santana* still in tow we start making a very wide turn to port to stop our converging course. Finally, when only four miles separate us from him, we hear his radio call asking us for our position.

If you are trying to avoid pirates, announcing your position on the radio is not very safe, but it may be a lot safer than being run down by a big ship. So we give him our position, and start to alter our course, but because of our tow we have to do so very slowly.

No sooner have we turned off the autopilot, and made a quarter turn to port when the ship finally starts to turn as well, but wait, he's turning the wrong way! Any turn is better than no turn, and we continue our slow turn, doing a complete circle. A different tactic to be sure, but we do manage to keep out of his way in doing so.

By mid morning the pale, sandy colored hills of Yemen appear ahead in the morning mist. This is what the Arab nations of the Mideast must look like. We search the hillsides over for the camel caravans that will surely appear out of the brown haze.

A fairly large-sized town is stretched along the waterfront at the foot of eroded sandstone hills with huge boulders looming above, looking as if they will come crashing down in the next rainstorm. But this village has been here beneath these boulders for centuries, so I guess it never rains. Also the filth on the sides of the main street attests to the lack of a good cleansing rain.

There must not be room under the rocky hill for a sewage treatment plant, for the harbor looks bad and certainly smells bad as well. The people are friendly, with several speaking English, and when we tell them we are from America, they are glad to meet us even though Yemen sided with Iraq during the Gulf war.

After a very short friendly visit by the customs people, the easiest clear in we have ever had, Stu takes the women into the town while Matt and I work on getting his engine's overheating problem solved. After much searching we find that the gasket on the plastic raw water strainer was allowing more air into the strainer than water. That fixed, we schedule an early morning departure for Djibouti.

We up anchor before 8 a.m. Yet another rally boat, *Blues,* a boat our size joins us. They have been in Al Mukalla for three days, resting and taking on fuel. It is a calm and windless day, so with all jerry cans refilled, we turn on our engines and head offshore once again.

Our tiny fleet is now in the most critical area in the world for sea pirates. The Yemen Island of Socotra is due south of us. A yacht had been raked with bullets from an assault rifle, and then boarded by pirates just the month before off the Yemen coast. Several commercial ships had been boarded in this area as well. And just to make things extra exciting, we get word from one of the other rally boats three days ahead of us that a 300-foot steel ship with lots of men lining the decks approached them in a threatening way. Only when the other three yachts headed back toward the threatened yacht did the ship bear off, and leave the area.

With this danger in mind we all are keeping an eye open for any unusual threat that might be approaching. About three hours out of Al Mukalla, we get an excited call on the VHF from Stu of *Stampede,* "Hey! I see WHALES ahead." Sure enough up ahead there are several waterspouts erupting in the air.

We are about a half a mile behind *Stampede,* and we can see that they seem to be surrounded by whales blowing. We also see a big one a hundred yards off our starboard beam moving along parallel with us blowing as he goes. After several minutes his head plunges forward, his mighty tail lifts out of the water, and down he goes into the briny deep.

Stampede actually had three within 20 feet of the boat and one swam along under the boat for a few minutes. That's a whale of an encounter for sure. Stu thinks they were right whales.

We have gotten ourselves smack dab in the middle of the shipping channel and big dark ships are passing us on both sides. We now spend several hours dodging ships, or having them dodge us. It looks to us that *Stampede* also has a ship within 100 yards at one time during the night. Now a 60-foot whale next to the boat is one thing, but a 600-foot ship that close in the dark is quite another. It turns out that both of the crew aboard *Stampede* were asleep in the cockpit and never saw it go by.

The rest of the trip goes pretty much the same way, under motor mostly, still having to dodge passing ships in the night. We arrive in Djibouti, Africa, at 10 o'clock in the morning. Everyone of us is extremely happy to have safely completed this long, dangerous rally leg. All of us in our little fleet of three are greeted heartily by the whole Millennium Rally fleet assembled in the harbor. It is a fine finish to a very unusual crossing.

22

The African World of Djibouti

We expected that Africa would be different, but now to see close up just how differently they live in this part of the world is indeed an eye opener.

The city of Djibouti, located in the Republic of Djibouti, is similar to Cochin, India and Galle, Sri Lanka without the tuk tuks in the streets, but with almost as many people walking or just sitting along them. At least Djibouti streets have sidewalks, and no open sewer ditches with ugly, gray yuck running in them.

Our fleet is at anchor in front of a nice yacht club overlooking the big commercial harbor that is handy to the city. Djibouti is a city of probably 25,000 people who are mostly Africans with many Middle Easterners of Arabic roots, and about 3,500 French nationals—down from 30,000 when it was a French possession attached to the military base here.

The local people are tall and slender with angular facial features more Arabic shape, and more delicate-looking than the full-faced blacks of the U.S. They are not as friendly as the people of other countries that we have visited, except for the moochers and beggars, and there are plenty of those. The local citizens probably have too many worries on their minds to be friendly.

We leave our boat in care of *Stampede's* Joe, and the crews of *Pimalo, Stampede,* and *Que Sera* take a three-day-tour out into the hills of Djibouti to see firsthand how the native population lives.

We are picked up from our respective boats by an outboard-powered launch and head to the town of Tadjourah with its 2,000-year-old water well ten miles across the Gulfe De Tadjoura. This is the second largest city in the whole country of Djibouti, and it reminds us all of what Dodge City must have looked like back some 130 years ago. The main street is paved, but the rest are stones and dirt. Some places look like time passed them by. Tadjourah is indeed ancient-looking and timeless.

Several men are building a large 100-foot-wooden fishing boat on the beach close to the bay, while the fishermen, in much smaller fishing boats, are unloading their catch onto the rocky beach which serves as the local fish market. Just back from the beach is an open-air butcher shop with mostly goat meat hanging from the rafters where birds sit and flies swarm. The women of the village are gathered all around pointing out which chunk they want for dinner that evening.

We are all loaded into a brand new four-wheel drive Toyota van and after a short tour of the town of about 2,000-3,000 people and four large Muslim mosques, we head for the hill country.

The road along the water is flat with lots of dry, brown trees and shrubs, and no grass at all because it is the dry season. Anywhere there is a well, or has ever been a well, there is a small village.

These tribesmen are living in one room stone-walled dwellings with a palm frond thatched conical roof or a round palm-frond woven mat domed building. We stop at one of the woven dwellings, and are allowed to go inside. The interior is of bent tree limbs forming very graceful arches over which the outside covering of palm mats are laid. Most of the room is taken up by a large platform formed with tree branches. This is a raised sleeping area.

Other than the goat herds, which everyone in the village seems to have, there is nothing else to eat or sell. They appear to have no other means of attaining money to buy other food staples, and it is too dry to grow vegetables.

The women all have many layers of colorful cloth wrapped around them from head to foot. The men wear a one-piece wrap that extends from their hips to near their ankles, and a regular collar type shirt.

About a half-hour out of the town the driver pulls off onto a dirt track. We follow a one-vehicle-wide trail for about 45 minutes, and in that time we see one small village, and a few more skinny camels.

Finally after bumping along a washed-out track, we pull into a small valley with a village of 12 native huts, plus one larger cement block building that appears to be relatively new.

We get out to stretch and are looking at a tame small antelope, when we notice they are unloading our gear from the car. This is the Sheraton where we're staying for the night.

We are shown our own individual round hut, and are told to rest up and lunch will be served in an hour. We check out our hut and ours is just lovely. One big bed made up of two big logs is held up off the concrete floor by four big boulders. On top of these two logs are laid about a dozen smaller tree branches all lashed together with goat hide thongs, and on top of that is a thin palm frond mat also bound with goat hide thongs still with their hair on them. Over this was a clean sheet, and a good heavy knit blanket. We brought our own pillows and towels.

No shelves, or chest of drawers, no sink, no chairs, or windows for ventilation and only a cloth drape covering the very small low entry.

And no toilet either. We are shown the co-ed outhouse with one toilet without a seat. A sink with no pipes attached to the drain is where one can his wash hands and feet at the same time, outside by the back wall of the new cement block building.

Our round building is made of many tree branches standing on end, with one end on the floor, the other under the roof, and lashed together with vines. The roof looks like a giant coolie hat made of sticks and vines. Needless to say there are lots of gaps between the many crooked branches so this building looks more like a beehive than a cabin, but then we didn't need a window for ventilation either with all those gaps. There is a palm frond interwoven wrapping all the way around the inside of the hut about four feet high, offering some privacy.

After scouting out our lodgings, we all meet in another more solid round stone walled hut with open areas in which to gaze out over our village. Here we sit and discuss our new lodgings which literally are a trip back in time, and wait for lunch with some concern.

After lunch we take a three-hour hike out into the bush. We climb up and down the many hillsides, and then way up a nearly dry riverbed to see a small waterfall. It is really just a trickle for it has been months since the last rain. The hike completed, we return to our village for a nice meal of tender boiled goat. Lois is sure that we have just eaten the small goat that we had seen in a cage near the kitchen earlier in the day. With unsettled stomachs we are given kerosene lanterns to take to our stick huts for much needed sleep after a trip to the now dark outhouse.

Sleeping on a two-inch thick pad laid on top of sticks probably isn't going to be a trip highlight. We are tired, so off we go to bed, hoping that due to lack of rain, we won't have too many mosquitoes coming in through the leaky stick walls.

Water is the key ingredient to survival here. This village has a spring in close proximity. So even in the dry season—most of the year—they have water. With this water they can do some local small field irrigation. This allows them to grow vegetables and fruits as well, and it provides water for the animals.

Each village has a herd of goats, usually a camel or two, some chickens, and a really well-off village may have a few cows. We see a herd of about a dozen cattle in the bottom of a valley that makes us wonder how they can ever survive, for it seems that there is no grass, straw, or even leaves on bushes that they can possibly eat. We wonder how any life can survive here.

So much for the life in the village. Off we go to see the rift line in the volcano-wrenched land at the west end of Tadjourah Bay. It is here that the great continent of Africa is beginning to split in two. We see the jagged tear through the volcanic rock up and down hills, across the highway, and even stand where they have seismographic equipment to measure its progress.

Then we travel onto their great salt lake. We miss the daily camel caravan that carries 500 pounds of salt on each camel from the lake to the city market, but we drive right out on what seems like a white, snowy beach during an Ohio winter. But it is pure tiny grains of salt that can be scooped up in your hands and eaten. It is that clean.

On the two-hour van trip back to Djibouti, we stop at a beach where the driver pulls out an awning, throws down blankets, and proceeds to serve us lunch out of the back of his van. This is our Sheraton restaurant. As we travel on, we see several nomadic tribes moving their few goats through the dry fields, and sometimes across the road in front of us. It seems to be an even tougher existence than the small village people have.

One hour out of Djibouti we pass the French military base, and can easily see why the tiny country of Djibouti is not being attacked by the Ethiopians like Eritrea. There are jets, helicopters, tanks, armored vehicles, and bunkers with machine gun emplacements placed all arourd the hills. It looks like the soldiers are on serious war-like maneuvers as we drive along the encampment.

We felt bad for these subsistence people trying to eke out a meager living in the dry hills, but what we see on the outskirts of the city of Djibouti is truly heart-wrenching. Hundreds of impoverished people are in squatters' camps all along the road, some in tents, some in makeshift corrugated tin boxes, and a lot of people just roaming around in the squalor. Many are refugees from Somalia and Ethiopia.

Additional people on the other side of the main road are simply villagers and nomads from the interior of Djibouti who have come to the city looking for work. There is none, but they can't go back home.

I don't think that this way of life for these people has changed much for several centuries. Djibouti is somewhat developed, but the rest of this small country is just as it has been since time began.

In the city all along the roads on both sides are trucks in line, bumper to bumper waiting for ships to unload food and medical supplies from various countries for delivery to both Somalia and Ethiopia. They cannot unload it fast enough to get it trucked ahead for the starving people awaiting it.

We have had our little taste of Africa, and are glad to be setting sail on the clean and quiet sea again.

23

The Two Faces of the Red Sea

The fleet has been assembled in Djibouti, Africa for a week. Several of us have provisioned, fueled up, and stocked up with cartons of Marlboro cigarettes. The reason for the purchase of the Marlboros will be revealed later. We do not smoke aboard or anywhere else for that matter. But soon Marlboros will play a crucial role in our voyage.

Sea Gem, Pimalo, Stampede, and *Que Sera Sera* depart from the harbor and head north to the entry into the Red Sea. Because Djibouti is located at the western end of the Gulf of Aden, we must first pass through the very narrow straits of Beb el Mandeb to enter the Red Sea.

We certainly do not want to test our luck by transiting this narrow 10-mile-wide area in the dark of the night. With that in mind we leave Djibouti in the afternoon, and stop only seven miles out of port. Our charts show a large area of coral reefs with some narrow channels. This is known to be a great place for snorkeling, so all four yachts slowly thread their way in the channel to find a wide spot to drop anchor.

It is indeed a good anchorage, and after an hour swimming around the spectacular coral, we stop for dinner, none of us in any hurry to get underway. We should have hurried a little, for as we watch the sunset, the day transitions into night. Trying to find our way back out through the coral into the deep water in the dark turns out to be slow and tedious.

As planned after a night of motoring, we arrive at the straits just after sunrise, and pass through rapidly. On our port side we can see the shoreline of Eritrea, and on our starboard side Yemen is in plain view. We have been warned to sail in view of each other, and under no circumstances stop before Egypt.

If the Red Sea were located any other place than between the countries of Yemen, Saudi Arabia, Eritrea, and Sudan it would be a thriving tourist area. The water is crystal clear, and islands are scattered all along its length. There are many safe protected bays, and literally thousands of thriving coral reefs yet to be discovered.

Our fleet of four motors on in close formation. One rally yacht, however, did not. *Blues,* a 39-foot-yacht from our rally, with two young Spanish men aboard, stops at the Brothers Islands just inside the straits to do some diving. Sure enough, they are soon boarded by five men all carrying military rifles, a few in uniforms.

The leader of the group demands $5000 U.S. dollars. Others in the group demand blankets and their sleeping bags. While one crew member tries to convince them their sleeping bags are greatly needed, the other offers a glass of wine to the one in charge, and convinces him they have only 100 U.S. dollars on board.

The *Blues* crewmen give them the $100, but that isn't good enough so the men take what is not fastened down, which includes bottles of alcohol, binoculars and a radio. With that treasure under their arms, they get back in the small boat they had come in, and soon are gone. *Blues* wastes no time upping anchor, and getting the heck out of there. This is the same yacht that we found in the harbor at Al Mukalla, Yemen. They were told not to go to Yemen either.

We are about to learn a lesson while voyaging on the Red Sea. As we are motoring along on the third day northward on a smooth, calm sea, we hear from Harry, the owner of *Die Swaene,* that they have 30 knots of wind on the nose. They are a day and a half ahead of us or about 200 miles north; strange, for we are looking for some wind here.

Motoring all night, with our fuel supply running low, we head into Port Sudan to find more. We learn that this is a staging center for an Italian company chartering skippered scuba dive boats for Italians.

It is a rundown commercial port so we just drop anchor in the small harbor. We no more than get our anchor set when a man in a small outboard boat comes alongside, and in very good English offers his assistance in getting fuel. He suggests that we stay aboard, for if we come ashore, we will have to go to customs and immigration, and that it will take at least two, probably three days to clear in and out.

So the man takes five of our empty jerry cans ashore and places them next to 15 or more sitting waiting for a truck to come and pick them up. I am just a little nervous about what will happen to those tanks when they disappear, and if they do return, I wonder what the contents will be. We had gotten some thick black diesel fuel in Cochin, India, which took a lot of filtering to clean, so we certainly did not want a repeat.

Our Sudanese helper brings us some fresh tomatoes and a couple of huge grapefruits, so we invite him aboard. We sit for an hour listening to him explain what bad things are happening to his country under the present ruler. He had been an engineer working in Germany, and had come home to visit his family. Once home, the officials took his passport away, and he can't go back to his job in Germany. There are few engineering jobs in Sudan.

He says that he is a trapped man living in a country that is heading in the wrong direction. Eighty-nine percent of the children attended a school 12 years ago, but now only the children of the military attend school. Most men do not have jobs, unless they are in the military, and there are no longer free elections in the country. It was a sad tale, told by a sad man.

The truck appears just before nightfall, and soon all of the tanks are gone. This is a calm, quiet night, one that should have been good for some serious sleep, but it was not. First, as night descends, the shadows stretch out longer and longer from the big Italian charter boats, making them seem surreal, like ghost ships sitting on a mirror. Then the insects on shore begin to hum, and chirp. We had been at sea for three days, and all we had heard was the water streaming past us as the motor droned on continuously. In a word everything is strange. Strange land, strange sounds, strange ever-slowly changing forms and shapes.

The next morning at eight the truck reappears on the shore, and the tanks are off loaded into our evening visitor's boat, and promptly brought out to us. We quickly dump the fine, clear fuel into our near empty tank, and ready for departure. By 8:30 our anchor is up, and with our new friend waving a sad farewell, we make our way back to the calm waters awaiting us on the Red Sea.

Que Sera is motoring along once again, and we are wondering if we will run out of fuel before we arrive in Safaga, Egypt, our first scheduled stop, 475 miles away. The motoring stops just before noon as a breeze fills in from the nor nor west at 10 knots.

By 1600 hours it's blowing 14 on the nose, and we are on a port tack under our headsail and double-reefed main heading quickly for Saudi Arabia. By 2000 hours we have tacked over to starboard away from the eastern shore. The wind is now down to ten knots. This would be a fine night for sailing for we have a bright full moon overhead, but the winds continue to head us. At 2330 hours I turn on the engine and furl in the headsail to get a better angle on our course, and to make way against the nose-on sharp waves.

By daybreak Lois is bashing against big waves generated by the 14 to 16 knots winds. We are still having fun though, for there is a large woodpecker-looking bird flying around us trying to find a place to land. He must not have liked this wind on his nose either.

Day two finds us now under a double reefed main, staysail, and our good old Denny, chugging along at 1500 rpm, still bashing and tacking to and fro across the angry sea. The winds rise to 18 and the waves follow suit, and we are taking large amounts of salty spray aboard.

Day three arrives and the wind dies to zero. Somehow we have caught up with *Pimalo*. We call them up on the VHF radio, and chat about our past days' miseries. As we are talking, we get a call from Thomas of *Polly* saying that they have found a safe bay on the western shore just inside the Egyptian border, and to come join them. We'll surely do just that, for we are ready for a rest.

Pimalo agrees, and we lead the way into the anchorage, and find not only *Polly,* but *Ginger* and *Nosy B* as well at anchor. This is, again, a strange and forbidding place to be. We had just come from the lands of Malaysia, and Thailand where all is green and lush. Here everything is sandy, brown and barren. There are no trees, and not even a stray camel to be seen on the shore. No sign of life is probably a good thing after the *Blues* experience.

We are out of there at first light, and glad to be gone. We never should have stopped, for now the wind is back to 20 knots from where it is we want to go, DAMN! Back up come the double-reefed main and the little staysail, plus the motor to bash northward.

Ginger, an Amel 48, set no sail, and is motoring straight into the teeth of the wind and waves. We choose to tack, getting help from all this wind. We tack toward Saudi Arabia quartering the waves. We held the port tack for three hours, and then tack over on starboard tack, each time crossing the freighter lanes.

After holding that tack for three hours we see another sailboat bashing head to wind without sails; it is *Ginger*. They certainly are tough sailors, for by now I would have had my left eye, and at least three teeth knocked out, it is so bad.

Looking back, this is about the same latitude that *Die Swaene* had reported strong winds and big seas. Further proof of an invisible wind line here is that at the evening SSB radio schedule, those yachts still a day behind us are all motoring with no wind at all. Twenty four knots in the face is plenty, and so we are now reefed down to the third reef in the main, staysail, and the engine now is at 1800 rpm to keep us moving slowly northward.

Night is falling on our twelfth day out of Djibouti, and the harbor at Safaga beckons us. We are very glad that rally control still has someone at the docks to talk us in, even at 2130 hours, for we are beat up and very tired.

The next morning we motor to an anchorage a couple of miles north of the commercial harbor, and drop two hooks in 100 yards of a sandy beach. Here we rest and lick our wounds, eat at a nice restaurant ashore, and take a tour bus across the desert to the city of Luxor on the Nile River.

I could fill a book with words describing the many treasures of Luxor: the magnificent Karnack Temple with its eerie and awesome light show and the spectacular Valley of the Kings burial grounds.

A large fleet of rally yachts depart Safaga together in the late afternoon on our way to Port Suez 248 nautical miles away. Light air greets the fleet of six yachts, so we motor along serenely.

The serenity lasts until midnight, and by 0200 hrs. it is blowing 20 plus from the northwest. I don't care, for it's Lois's turn on watch, and my turn in the sack. Fat chance, for she sends me forward to the mast in the dark of the night to slip a couple of reefs in the main. Once again we are blasting to windward with salt spray all over us, not fun at all.

The next day we enter into the narrow Gulf of Suez. We are still punching into the wind, but the waves are not as steep, so we are making much better time. We find an island half way up the gulf, and drop our anchor off Marsa City. Here we get another good night's sleep even though the wind is still howling through the rigging at 20 plus.

The anchor is up early (0515) the next morning only to find still more fresh air hurling itself at us from the northwest. By noon we are seeing steady winds of 25 with gusts to 30. We are still tacking with reefed main and staysail, plus a little engine to get additional headway. Suddenly the wind is down to ten. Even better the crashing waves are gone as well. It's only 15 miles to Port Suez.

We are beat once again; sleep comes early at anchor in front of the Suez Yacht Club. We have run the Red Sea gauntlet. Lois says that if our voyage had started with this Red Sea challenge, she would have gone directly back to land in Ohio. Most of the fleet participants tour Cairo and visit the pyramids; we decide to tour our bunks.

The next day we have the brown salt crust washed off the boat, at a price of $10 for the water. We don't use much, but at least most of the boat is clean again.

We take on our Suez pilot, Zeckle Hamaab, and with three other yachts we head up the famous Suez Canal. No sails allowed. Our pilot is a polite young man who takes the helm for most of the trip as he describes the job and responsibilities of a canal pilot.

At noon he takes time off for his prayers. He asks if he can go below to say his prayers. Sure, be our guest. We have a carpet on the sole, a fine silk carpet purchased in Singapore, but he pushes it aside, and takes one of our thick bath towels, and lays it on the floor. He washes his hands and feet, kneels down on the towel, and prays with his head down for at least ten minutes. I think I'm a good Christian, but this is real religious dedication.

We motor fast to get to Lake Timsch where we anchor just off the commercial docks. Our pilot, with a carton of our Djibouti Marlboros, a hat from Australia, and a Corona beer tee shirt for his expectant wife, gets off here.

In the morning a second pilot is brought out to us aboard *Prinz Karl,* and we proceed out the bay toward the canal. Just before we reach the canal, our pilot asks us to stop. We stop, we wait, and we wait some more.

After at least an hour of waiting, a huge ship's bow appears from behind the low hills to our north. It gets bigger and bigger and nearly fills the entire gap between the hills and the island to our starboard. There is a sea-going tug in front of it and a second one at its stern. It must be six or seven stories high. It is most definitely a 1,500-foot super oil tanker. Our pilot explains that it has paid millions of dollars to run empty through the canal, and that this is the first one ever to do so.

Off we go back onto the Suez, which is now a 42-mile straight-line ditch through the desert. Boring would be the word here as one can not see past the high sand banks on both sides of the ditch-canal. Nothing but blue sky overhead, blue water straight ahead and behind, with nothing but brown sand everywhere else.

We arrive in Port Said, and our pilot is picked up by a small motor launch with a crew of four. Here go the rest of our Marlboros. This is an episode of old world haggling. We gave the pilot his obligatory carton of cigs, but now the crew of the launch wants their portion as well. So I give one man one pack. Then he asks for a pack for each of the other crewmen, so OK here are three packs. "Well," he says "I must have three packs for the captain." "OK, here are three more packs."

All this time we are motoring along at five knots with their launch tied very firmly to us. The pilot, who has his whole carton out of sight in his duffel bag, announces that he must have more for the immigration officials or they will stop us further down the river. A few more are handed up from below deck, but I make a mistake of giving him two packs more than I had given the crew of the launch attached to us. They didn't detach. Yet another hand comes out demanding more packs of Marlboros.

My, my, this is getting rather tight here, for we only held back two packs from our original three cartons. Hoping for the best with no further demands downstream, we hand over our last two packs. It works; with the now fully-stocked crew smiling at us, they untie and speed off across the fast flowing Nile River. We heard that the Suez Canal has been renamed—the Marlboro Canal. Now we know why.

24

Rome, The Return of the Flame

Every sailor worth his salt dreams of sailing the beautiful and historic Mediterranean Sea, and here it is passing under our keel. At 1615 hrs. we pass the mile-long breakwalls of the entrance to the Suez; with all sails up and pulling, we are headed northwest to Crete 420 miles away. As we embark on this dark wine sea, we are experiencing some strong, mixed emotions.

We are glad to be free of the Red Sea, the Suez, and the pirates, yet here we are on another unknown sea that stretches vaguely ahead of us. Yet isn't that our life in this world—every new day is another new adventure?

Lois and I are anticipating the culmination of the Millennium Odyssey Rally in Rome when members of the fleet will hand the flame lit in Jerusalem at Jesus' tomb to Pope John Paul II during Easter week. What a moment that will be. But we are also aware that we will soon be saying farewell to fellow sailors with whom we have shared a great camaraderie as we voyaged on the oceans of the world and reached out to people in many lands.

This sea is dark. No stars. No moon. It is dark. I hate to wake Lois, but she pops out of the companionway right on time and takes over the watch. I linger for awhile so that she can get oriented, but after 15 minutes she exclaims that she cannot see anything. What should she do, she asks. I'm tired and a little smug for I'm going to bed; so pointing to the lifelines on both sides of *Que Sera Sera*, I tell her, "Honey, just keep us between the white lines, and we will be fine."

At day break we are motoring along with the wind down to two knots. After the thrashing we took on the Red Sea, motoring along on a flat, calm sea is just fine with us. Fine until noon when the wind fills in from the northwest. Our GPS course to Crete is 306 degrees, northwest. We're a sailboat so we sail west at 240 degrees.

The longer the wind blows and the seas become sloppy, and choppy, our speed diminishes proportionately. For the first time since we left Chile in February of 1999, we are cold. All the warm clothes are packed deep down out of reach in a closet.

Day after day the wind blows from the northwest, and we must slog on. First to the west, then to the north, then to the west, tacking our way slowly towards Crete. The winds are never above 20 knots, but even if the wind is OK, the sea keeps bashing against us, impeding our forward progress.

Since it is only early April, we should not be looking for hot weather this far north. It seems we are the only ones out here sailing on the Mediterranean at this time of the year. But we are on a mission to get to Rome by Easter.

On comes the motor again as we round the northeastern end of the island of Crete. Night falls as we head due west along the north coast. Later we visit the town of Agios Nickolaos which is just what we pictured a small, Greek town would look like. It's built around a small pond off the main channel. The local colorful wooden fishing boats are tied along the harbor side, and there are many small restaurants overlooking the pond.

We spend ten days here being wined and dined by the officials. Ramon, the owner of *Aventurero III,* throws a big celebration bash for the rally fleet, where we count our blessings for being able to travel with so many wonderful people.

There is an official rally start on the last leg to Italy. As *Foxy Lady* and *Que Sera Sera* battle for first to start, the rest of the fleet crank up their iron sails, and motor at seven knots out of the bay.

The next morning the breeze fills in from the northeast, and we are able to hoist the big kite to make speed westward. By noon, however, we are approaching the western end of Crete when the sky begins to turn to a richer blue. We have been reading about the different weather systems here that stalk the unwary sailor. We douse the kite even though the wind is still only 10 to 12. It's a good thing we get it down, for not 10 minutes after the takedown, the wind has switched to the northwest, and is now blowing 25. That was close; God must be watching over us.

Our heading was supposed to be west-nor-west toward the Straits of Messina and the toe of Italy, but now we must beat into it and can only make it westward toward the south of Sicily. Bashing to windward for days is hard work, but thankfully we have the company of *Pimalo* nearby each day.

That night on watch, Lois has her most frightening experience of the whole trip. She is using the night scope to check to see if there is anything around that the radar is not picking up. Sure enough, she can see a huge ship which should have shown up on radar since it goes out 24 miles, but the radar screen is blank. She immediately gets on the VHF radio and calls, "Ship, ship this is sailing vessel *Que Sera Sera.* I am directly ahead of you. Are you passing to port or starboard?" NO ANSWER! "Freighter, freighter this is a sailboat directly ahead of you. Are you passing to port or starboard?" STILL NO ANSWER. She changes direction 20 degrees. The ship seems to be getting closer, and does not change direction. She calls again knowing that all ships must have an English speaking person on their radio.

At this point she rouses me to come determine what we need to do. Out of a deep sleep, I advise her to go another 20 degrees to starboard. As this ship gets larger, and still the radar shows nothing, she calls again. NO ANSWER.

At 5:15 as the sky lightens, a US aircraft carrier passes to port a football field length away. There is her answer; they don't want anyone to know that they are here, and they have scrambled our radar. They knew all along where we were through both radar and heat sensors.

As Lois and I piece together last night's incident, I reflect on my own crying out, not to a huge ship on a dark night, but to God who seemingly turned his back on us, and could not hear our pain when our son was killed. I knew somehow that God was there, but I couldn't communicate with him. As time has passed, we both have realized that God is always present and always listening, even in our darkest days and nights.

The morning of day four finds us motor sailing northward to the south of the instep of the Italian boot. And at noon we are having a quiet lunch in calm waters two miles off shore with both of us wearing big happy smiles to be out of the bashing sea.

Later, out on a glassy Tyrrhenian Sea, we motor straight northward past the island of Stromboli with an active volcano. We are now headed on to our final rally port, Civitavecchia, Italy.

Darkness falls as the motor drones on and on through a very dark night. It is a cold night, but one full of stars. It is our last night at sea, for tomorrow we will arrive in the port city of Civitavecchia and the official end of the Millennium Odyssey Rally.

Arriving in port, we are greeted by all of the other rally participants since we are the second to last to finish. Also present are Carol Jagel and her daughter, our special niece Julia; what a nice surprise. These two special family members and our son and daughter were part of the send-off group that saw us off from St. Augustine, Florida in 1998.

Three days later, the rally organizers host the closing awards dinner party at the local yacht club. The fine dinner is followed by the presentation of many awards. The last prize to be given is the "Spirit of the Rally Award." Lois and I are taken aback and deeply touched when we are called forward to be presented with such a meaningful award.

Later the members of the Millennium Rally are taken by special bus to Rome where we gather in Saint Peter's Square, with 2,000 other citizens of the world, for an audience with Pope John Paul II and the presentation of the flame.

It is a moving moment as Jimmy Cornell and our rally sponsor Senor Rafael Medina from the Canary Islands present Pope John Paul II a Millennium Rally lamp. This glowing lamp, lit at the Church of the Holy Sepulchre in Jerusalem 22 months earlier, had been carried to all the continents of the world as a fulfillment of Jimmy Cornell's vision to spread hope, peace and goodwill to people in 40 different cultures.

The Pope explains, in five different languages, what we have accomplished. Then following a tour of the Sistine Chapel, we have a small private audience with Cardinal Carlo Furno, the Grand Master of the Order of the Holy Sepulchre.

This is also a sad time because now the fleet of our sailing friends will be sailing off in all directions toward their respective home ports, or other far-off destinations.

We have become very close as only a group of sailors can during our year of traveling together. We have shared exciting travel destinations and sea conditions both good and bad. We've worked together on boat maintenance issues. We have eaten meals, celebrated often at parties, swam and played in oceans together, and now, together, we will experience the feeling of separation as we go on our different paths. We know we will most likely never see some of our friends again. But we will maintain contact with several as we meet again on other sailing journeys.

As we say goodbye, our friends, Alfredo and Nicoleta of the Italian yacht, *Jancriss,* are playing "Time To Say Goodbye" by Sarah Brightman and Andrea Bocelli on their stereo system on the rally dock. Talk about tugging on the heart strings.

Once again we must deal with loss, the loss of this wonderful group of sailing friends. We had already said goodbye to all of our good friends that we had sailed with for the first half of the rally in Australia. This is an emotional and painful time, yet it is also another beginning for us as well.

The amazing Millennium Odyssey Rally ends here for most of the participating yachts. There will be a final ceremony in London, completing the journey for those of us who started there.

Lois and Don standing in front of the wall world map where their ocean odyssey was recorded by their son, Fred, president of Babson Fluid Power, Inc. (center) and other employees and family.

Lois and her daughter, Dee Coghlan, at Dee's house where the Babsons stayed when returning home occasionally. They are holding a didgeridoo, an Australian Aboriginal instrument.

Don siphoned diesel fuel from the Big Blue Barrel while at sea.

Lois, after she administered rum to a freshly caught tuna, prior to preparation for the dinner meal on board Que Sera.

King Neptune and his lovely Mermaid celebrated in style as they crossed the equator.

Shaum Rami, an educated Sudanese native who spoke English, German, French as well as Sudanese, purchased fresh fruit and fuel for us. During a lengthy conversation, he described the difficult conditions in Sudan.

The lighting of the Millennium Odyssey lamp at the tomb of Jesus was the first time that a Roman Catholic priest and an Eastern Orthodox priest participated jointly in a religious ceremony.

The governor of Lanzarote in the Canary Islands signed the Babsons' log book following Don and Lois' first flame ceremony.

Grandson Nate received his own special prize on Awards Night for catching the biggest piece of coral on an anchor.

The entire Millennium Odyssey fleet assembled and dressed for church in Tonga

Lois as she sat on her log bed inside a woven circular stick hut at the Djibouti "Sheraton" in Africa.

We were welcomed to Bega Island, Tonga as the assistant chief prepared a kava root drink for us.

Exploring the *Mediterranean Sea*

The Mediterranean, The Atlantic and Home

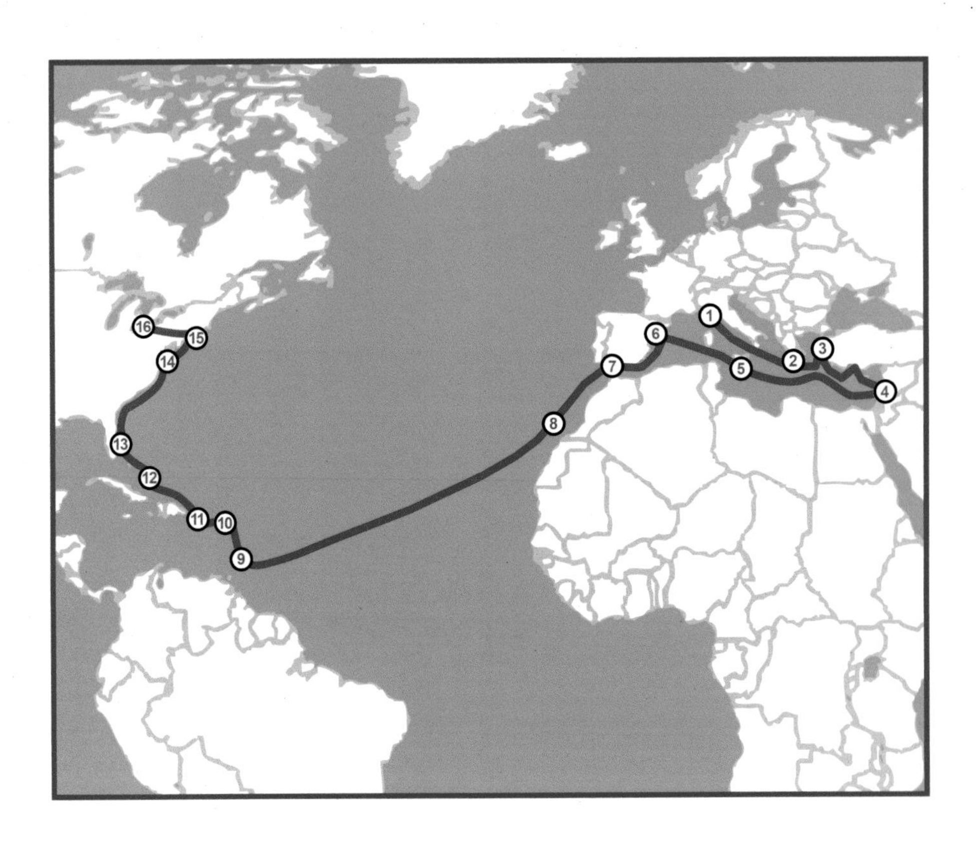

1. Rome
2. Greece
3. Turkey
4. Middle East
5. Sicily
6. Barcelona
7. Gibraltar
8. Canary Islands
9. Barbados
10. Virgin Islands
11. Puerto Rico
12. Bahamas
13. Florida
14. Chesapeake Bay
15. New York City
16. Home

25

The Romantic Mediterranean

The Millennium Odyssey Rally is over in Rome, Italy, but we plan to continue our exploration of the Mediterranean Sea and attend the final rally ceremony in London. With that thought in mind, we turn the bow of *Que Sera Sera,* our floating home, back to the east rather than to our home far away to the west. We have made arrangements to meet up with several friends prior to the Millennium Odyssey's end.

We had sailed right past the magical Isle of Capri as we hurried to Rome. We had been told of the beauty of the island of Kafallionia, one of the Greek Ionian Islands. The Corinth Canal is a must-do, and Athens, of course, so steeped in history, is an important stop as well. We are joined by Joe and Joette McDonald to sail the Cyclades in the Aegean Sea. This is the dream of so many sailors.

We enjoyed our short stay at Crete in April, so another stop there is mandatory as well. We knew that Teva and Hinano were waiting for us there. After two weeks of touring, and just enjoying Agios Nikolaos with our Tahitian friends, we leave *Que Sera Sera* and fly to London.

In London, we once again rejoin those fine friends of the fleet who had sailed around South Africa, and who had just completed their circumnavigation of the earth. This will be the final Millennium Odyssey event.

It is grand with Jimmy Cornell presiding and former British Prime Minister Sir Edward Heath in attendance. We enjoy a fine reunion with the crews of the six boats with whom we had left London in 1998. It is a special pleasure for Lois and me, not only for the fun and camaraderie, but to cheer when *Harmonie* takes first place for the Greenwich Rally Group. After parties, awards, and one last flame ceremony, we say farewell to this group of friends knowing that we will never see many of them again.

A few days later we hop the Chunnel train, which quickly whisks us under the English Channel to France. When we emerge back up from the dark tunnel, we speed through miles and miles of lush farm lands.

We continue on the train to Luxembourg to stay with our friends, Chris and Ern of *Pimalo,* who take us touring not only in Luxembourg, but on to Paris. We stay in a quaint four-story hotel near the heart of the city so we see all of the highlights. As the light of the sun dims, we hop aboard an evening cruise on the River Seine, a romantic, historic river.

Next we travel on to Switzerland. Our Ed had attended school in Lausanne in 1995, and had shared many stories, so we feel close to him as we see first hand what he described. After traveling 34,000 miles around the world at five knots, we find the fast scenic train rides exciting. Our next stop is Venice, Italy.

Boats of all shapes and sizes are picking up passengers to carry them across a small bay to this Medieval Mediterranean traders' nirvana—the most romantic boat afloat—a Venetian Gondola.

Now it is time to fly back to Crete, to our waiting floating home, *Que Sera Sera*. Once we do some re-provisioning, we take two months to cruise the Greek Islands. We head eastward to Rhodes, one of the Dodecanese Islands. These are lush, green islands with lots of well-protected bays in which to drop anchor. Each island has so much history. Rhodes for example has a walled crusader city, and Patmos is where the disciple John wrote the book of Revelation.

After a month of island-hopping the Greek Dodecanese Islands, we find ourselves in Kusadasi, Turkey, in the large Setur Marina. Here we have our *Que Sera Sera* (the Turkish people call her "Cute Sara Sara") hauled out and shored up on the ground with tree trunks under her hull. We are a little bit anxious about logs and tree limbs holding her up in this land of many earthquakes. While readying our boat for the winter, we take time to tour the Biblical sites of Ephesus, Miletus, Didyma, and Priene. We are so surprised at how much of the Bible's stories took place in Turkey.

By Thanksgiving, we head home to Ohio where we will stay in our new condo until April. People are often interested in hearing about our journey. The number one question asked is how we handled big storms. We can honestly say that we did what was necessary to stay safe. Often it's like a "Chinese firedrill," for a lot has to happen in a very short time. Afterwards comes the peace and stillness, allowing us to reflect on all we did.

We've also discovered grief is like that. When we had to face what had happened to Ed and its effect on our lives, we responded by going through the motions of what needed to be done.

On our trip our spirits have become still and peaceful for we've had so many quiet hours to reflect on our loss. Quiet hours on vast oceans, together. We are so glad God gave us a wonderful son to have for 32 years—he was truly a blessing. Now God has stilled the storms of our souls.

26

Return to the Sea and New Destinations

The allure of wind in our sails, currents flowing under our keel and places we've never seen, beckon. After a winter at home in Ohio, we fly back to Turkey, and re-float our little house, and set sail once more on the dark waters of the Mediterranean. After two weeks in Kusadasi, we join yet another rally— the EMYR- Eastern Mediterranean Yacht Rally. Being a part of a group of 47 other yachts allows us to do many things we would not attempt on our own.

We sail the coast of Turkey, going from one outstanding marina to another, and taking bus trips to see the many ancient places of the Greco-Roman periods.

From Turkey we sail to the old Roman seaport of Girne on the Turkish half of Cyprus where we visit the Biblical sights of Paphos and Salamis where Paul and Barnabas converted many to Christianity.

We also tour Syria, Lebanon, Israel, and Egypt. Syria is an arid, poor country, though we did enjoy Damascus, the crusader castle, Le Krac des Chevaliers, and the magnificent deserted city of Palmyra, one of the most famous archaeological sites in the Middle East.

We fall in love with Beirut which is one of the most beautiful cities. The plush marina in Jouniea just north of Beirut is the finest we have seen in all the world.

Next we stop in three different cities in Israel, each for a week of travel and sightseeing. We travel inland by coach to Jerusalem, the Sea of Galilee, and Herod's citadel Masada overlooking the Dead Sea.

We can't cross the Atlantic until November, so we still have four months to leisurely cruise. So back to Cyprus, but this time to the southern or Greek side of the island, where we rest up after the fast pace of the EMYR.

We live for a week in the old trading cities of Limassol and Larnaca before going back to Turkey. We revisit the many Greek Islands between Turkey and Crete where we left *Que Sera,* and do an Egyptian Nile cruise.

Later we coast hop along Sicily in the shadow of Mt. Etna and its active volcano to the historic city of Siracusa where we met Ann Harsh of *Harmonie* for land touring.

We spend three wonderful weeks in Barcelona—one of our favorite cities. We are having lunch with Javier and Barbara Visiers and Ramon, from the Odyssey Rally, when Ramon receives a phone call that a plane has flown into one of the World Trade Center towers. We are not too concerned at first because the translation from Spanish to English indicates that it is a small plane. Then only minutes later he receives a second call relating that a big, commercial plane had struck the second tower.

Disheartened and saddened, we say farewell to our friends and start walking back to our boat. We pause at a small bar and watch the picture play over and over again, showing the two planes striking the towers, and then the towers falling.

Standing in silence, we are dumbfounded. How could this possibly be happening? We have tickets to fly home for September 12th, and are all packed.

Sadness weighs heavily on our hearts. We can feel this sadness hanging heavy over the entire city. We find an Internet café in town to e-mail home our change in plans. We are deeply touched as we notice each monitor has a flowing American flag across a clear blue background, and the words "Our Condolences to the American People"

The magnitude of the disaster in New York is now sinking in. No planes will fly to the states until September 18th.

Our next stop is London to attend the wedding of a couple who had sailed on various boats in the Millennium Rally. L.J. Morgan from *Risque'*, and Zetty from *Happy Spirit*, are being married, and most of the fleet that had sailed to South America are there. And we thought we wouldn't see these people again. We have shared an experience that has made us close.

Home again on *Que Sera* in Barcelona we go back to the Balerics to cruise the rest of these outstanding islands. October is quickly coming to an end so we press eastward stopping along the Costa del Sol .

Our last stop is the vast rock of Gibraltar, the gateway to the deep waters of the Atlantic Ocean. Later we meet up with our Tahitian friends of *Prinz Karl* in the early morning hours, and head south and west to the Canary Islands—659 miles away.

We are escorted past Morocco by a female orca with her baby attached to her side. What an exciting way to enter the Atlantic.

We have a pleasant non-eventful sail to Lanzarote. There we meet our friends Charles and Saundra Gray on *Sea Gem* and celebrate New Year's Eve 2002 at a villa overlooking the ocean.

27

West to the New World

Que Sera Sera is finally heading west across the Atlantic. Our next port will be in the West Indies. We are leaving the Canary Islands in the company of two other sailboats, *Prinz Karl* and *Sea Gem*. The weather is unsettled, and several yachts are waiting for easterly winds, but we feel that we have been here long enough, and the winds, though 20 plus knots, will be from abeam as we head southwest to Barbados.

We slog to windward to clear Grand Canaria Island, but after an hour we turn to port, and start to sail free before the wind, all doing six or better knots. For the first two or three hours we sail until we enter the huge wind shadow of the very high mountainous center of Grand Canaria Island. The wind totally shuts off, and on comes our motors on a flat, calm sea.

Motoring a few miles is usually good, because it keeps the batteries charged, but this time it is not. The high temperature alarm shocks us out of our book reading just as we are starting to get a little wind back in our sails. We promptly shut down our ever-faithful Denny Diesel, and set all sails again. Not long after, we are out of the wind shadow of the mountain, and are beam reaching in 20 knots of wind, and the seas that had been building for four days are making our ride a little rough, especially for the guy working in the hot engine room replacing the raw water impeller.

I'm not sure why we started the generator, Little Denny Genny, but after it runs maybe 15 minutes it chugs to a stop also. We have plenty of wind so on we sail past three more of the Canary Islands with the seas getting bigger and bigger as we go.

We probably could sail all the way across the ocean without a way to charge our batteries. Christopher Columbus was able to do it, but he didn't have a fridge to make ice for our afternoon cocktails, nor did he have an electric autopilot to steer his boat, nor did he have any other boat traffic on the sea that requires navigation lights. We, however, must be able to generate electricity, but after two hours of working next to a hot engine our mechanic emerges slightly seasick, and asks the mate if we can head for a calm place to get things sorted out.

"Sure, honey," comes her reply, "But we are 25 miles past El Hierro, the last island! Do you want to turn back?" " Yeah, we better," comes the somewhat sour reply. "At six knots we can be there before dark."

We do turn back after a VHF radio call to the other two boats, *Prinz Karl* and *Sea Gem* who turn back as well. We didn't make it before dark.

Here we are trying to find a little bay shown on the chart as a good anchorage in the dark of the night, in the rain, with wind over 30 knots blasting us. This is one time our trusty radar pays off because we can tell just how close the over-hanging cliffs are off our bow. Too close! So we bail out and continue farther around to the north of the island.

On the north side of El Hierro we are in the shadow of a pretty big mountain, and a calm sea. The mate is at the helm with a double-reefed mainsail only, tacking back and forth in the bay in the catabolic winds off the mountain.

I'm back in the engine rooms below. I get the impeller replaced on the main engine, and fire it up successfully, but I cannot revive the generator, even enough to get a put put out of it. I would like to have stayed in the bay overnight, but with periodic blasts of wind of over 40 knots down the mountain and the bay being a caldera formed by a volcano, there is no safe anchorage. With our stalwart friends, we turn southwest and head once again to the new world— 3,200 miles away.

It is a long night worrying about how we will keep the batteries charged if the engine overheats again, but with a strong east wind we are making seven knots straight towards Barbados. Helping us get through the night is the sight of *Prinz Karl's* masthead light a half a mile behind us. What great friends. We lost 12 hours while I got the engine running, and they have stuck with us.

The next day we run the engine for over seven hours slowly bringing the battery back up from the negative 185 amps that it had reached during the night. We also deploy our water drag generator behind the stern, but get little input from that. But it is fun to watch as it churns along 100 feet behind just under the surface of the water, and even occasionally jumping clear out of the face of some of the steeper waves.

On the fourth day out of the Canaries, we think that our drag propeller is going to become whale food. Shortly after lunch, a 30-foot long minke whale comes swimming by only about ten feet away. In a blink of an eye, he is alongside *Que Sera Sera* and then down and under us he goes. Maybe that's not good. Nothing bad happens though, as he surfaces on the other side of us without a bump, to spout and take a breath. He hangs around for two hours after a little spy hop to look us over. Our whale appears for the next six days, spending time with us until one of the two freighters we saw on the passage passes nearby. We think our whale is headed back northeast with him. The morning our whale friend does not appear alongside us is especialy hard. Any loss of friends seems to deeply hurt us, and this loss of this whale deeply affected us as well. The day seems extra gray, and the clouds seem to hang suspended motionless over us.

Without our finned distraction we have time to reflect on the fact that our fabulous sailing adventure is coming to a close, and that soon the realities of what lies ahead at home will be facing us.

Questions like what will we do about our fluid power business that we had left behind in the care our son and son-in-law? Will we go back to work? Will we return to our upscale condo? And of course the big question is how will we get along at home without our Eddie. We had snow skied, and sailed with Ed yearly. We had partied and gone to Browns football games with Ed, and had for a few years even been in business with him. With all of those thoughts swirling around in our heads, we sail westward.

Abruptly, we are jolted out of our reverie as we lose a cherished old friend—our big black, yellow and white asymmetrical spinnaker. Gone with the wind in the dark of the night. Lois told me to take it down at sunset, but we had flown it all night the previous night with winds never exceeding sixteen knots. We were trying to keep up with a 53-and a 54-footer, and we can with our trusty kite so I said not to worry about it, it will be all right. Wrong!

Just a little short of midnight a ripping sound is heard above the 18 knots sometimes 19 knots of howling winds. Because of the black and white color of the sail we can easily see it even on a dark night, but when I look forward, all I see is black. It is gone. The middle is gone, but looking up to the top, some pieces are still blowing in the wind.

"Honey!" An urgent voice is heard in the dark, "We have a problem with the kite. Can you please come help me?"

My mate appears quickly, and springs into action helping me drag the shredded sail back on the deck. This is our fourth time having to haul it back on board from the briny deep blue sea. We have it out of the water in a few minutes.

We find out later from a sailmaker in St. Thomas, U.S. Virgin Islands,that the sail is unrepairable because the sailcloth has deteriorated. His exact words were "You should feel good you wore the sail out; not many people wear out a sail, especially a spinnaker." So I guess we got our money's worth out of it; still it was a sad day for us when we put that wonderful sail in the dumpster.

The next day, shortly before noon, we see a big sea-going tug approaching from astern. Not long after the sighting, the tug hails us on the VHF radio. "What are two small sailboats doing out here in these big seas? Where are you headed?" "Barbados," is our reply. "Do you need water, fuel, or food?" he asks. "No, but how about a tow?" I reply.

"Well, I could certainly do that, but I'm afraid that the owners of this tug would send you a bill, a very large bill if I did," was his reply. We quickly withdrew our request, needless to say.

We have 20 to 25 knots of wind from directly behind us, and are going wing and wing with the headsail on a pole. *Sea Gem,* having no pole with which to hold out their headsail, has their spinnaker out, and sail sometimes to the south, sometimes to the west, but could not sail straight to the southwest, so they soon are a day behind us. Every morning, soon after sunrise we spot *Prinz Karl*. We talk back and forth several times a day on the VHF radio, and twice a day on the SSB long-range radio to *Sea Gem*.

Since our little generator is inoperable, we can not make water, so for the first time in our voyage, we have to conserve our water supply in our three tanks which hold almost 200 gallons. The best way to cut back is to greatly limit our daily shower to one very short one every three days.

We are probably getting a little stinky when we were blessed by an hour long gentle, warm rain 15 days out of the Canaries. Here is plenty of water so we cast aside our clothes, grab our soap and shampoo, and head out on the foredeck, giggling like little kids in the rain. As the rain falls, we proceed to shower in the water provided from the vast gray heavenly sky above. Our faces are wreathed in smiles as we soap each other's slippery body—what fun!

Prinz Karl stays within sight part of each day, but as the sun set on our last night, they did not reef down for the night as we did, and by morning we feel like the only boat on this big blue ocean.

After 19 days and 18 nights we spy the hills of Barbados ahead as we watch them slowly grow taller. And all around us we are being welcomed by scores of flying fish. Large 10 and 12-inch long ones at first, and then by squadrons of smaller and then even smaller ones. They skitter in silvery blue streaks away in all directions from the plunging bow of our boat as if leading our way into this fabled seafarers' landing place in the new world. And so with a fishy fanfare we arrive safely at the shores of Barbados and the Caribbean Sea.

Prinz Karl beat us in by three hours, but we beat *Sea Gem* in by 23 hours. The three boats are reunited at a small marina resort complex in Barbados where we all celebrate our successful crossing at the resort dining room with a beautiful meal and a glass of fine red wine.

28

Returning Home

Sea Gem turns south while *Prinz Karl* and *Que Sera* continue northward up the windward chain, island hopping to Guadeloupe. Shortly, *Prinz Karl* must turn east. We have become very close with Teva and Hinano as we have sailed with them since our meeting in Tahiti a year and a half ago. Dry eyes don't come easy when you see a friend's boat sail over the horizon.

Because we try to approach life with an openness and a welcoming spirit, we are continually blessed with many friendships, both of short and long duration. As we travel, we are joined by several friends who accompany us on our journey home.

Onto the Leeward Islands and the lovely island of Antigua where the Morgans of *Risqué* come aboard to sail to St. Thomas in the American Virgin Islands. The Morgans depart as our son Fred and his family join us to sail the British Virgin Islands. It is so good for us to spend time in the sun and sea with them.

After they fly out, we head toward Georgetown in the Bahamas some 1,000 miles almost due west. We pick up our sailing friend Ken Watt in Puerto Rico and are joined in the Turks and Caicos by his wife Rhonda and daughter, Kristin.

After celebrating Easter in these special islands, they fly out and our friends, Dan and Karen Somes of Vero Beach, Florida, come aboard to sail the rest of the way to Georgetown in the Bahamas. The Somes leave and a day later we are joined by Ralph and Ann on *Harmonie,* who have sailed from Ft. Lauderdale to voyage with us through the Bahamas.

After a pleasant crossing of the Gulf stream, we arrive in Ft. Pierce just in time for dinner ashore. As we are seated and glance at the menus, Lois begins to cry. Huge sobs and crocodile tears.

"Honey, what is the matter?" I ask. "I don't want our trip to come to an end, and I want everything on this menu, it all looks soooo good." Bring this gal a Manhattan; she is losing it!

After two weeks heading northward on the lovely Intercoastal Waterway, we are in the Chesapeake Bay. This also is a waterway full of fun and interesting places to visit and so we cruised here with friends Vivian and Rob Skladan from Vermilion, aboard.

After a two-day stop in Cape May to spend time with Jack and Sue McAfee who did the EMY Rally with us on *Kismet,* we were off on a calm North Atlantic Ocean to Sandy Hook and New York Harbor.

We had sailed across three of the oceans of the world—one of them three times. We had sailed upon seven of the major seas into hundreds of bays and even up a few rivers.

We had met so many friendly people of many different cultures, races and religions. We'd visited fascinating far-off cities and towns. We'd encountered many people who spent their entire lives in the same city or little towns. By doing so, we discovered we are very much alike in our needs and desires. So with that small insight into our magnificent world, we continue on up the mighty Hudson River back to Huron, Ohio to end our voyage on the oceans of the world.

We had continually embraced new friends from all parts of the world, and let them go as we voyaged to separate destinations. This is the way life is. This is the lesson that we had to learn as we tried to cope with our son Eddie's sudden departure.

During our sailing odyssey of five years, we had slowly reclaimed our lives as we journeyed on the seas through our grief. We know grief still lingers. The empty hole in our lives will always be with us. But as God heals our pain, we have learned to count our many blessings. Our greatest blessing is our wonderful family—our daughter, Dee; our son, Fred, and their spouses, and our five grandchildren. Our experience of loss has made us more aware of how precious the lives of the people we love are.

We have no fear of death for Ed awaits us. Our faith has been tested by our loss, but it is stronger, for our strength has come from God. We have an awesome God and we often say we are the luckiest unlucky people because we have been privileged to see his many creations throughout the world.

Can human beings escape loss? No, we can't escape loss—not the loss of a son, not the loss of parents, not the loss of good friends. Loss will always be there. As we sailed away, virtually around the world, trying to ease our loss, we found healing. And we have come to understand that when someone you love becomes a memory, that memory becomes your treasure.

Sail On

We've seen some stormy seas, some knotted lines,

some moments when recaulking was required.

We've had some days when we just lay becalmed,

felt the journey was not all that we'd desired.

A wiser hand was at the wheel to guide us,

to teach us when to come about, to tack.

He helped us realign our heading

so we would have a fair wind at our back.

The voyage now is mostly joyful sailing

with sunlight and a gentle, steady breeze.

How blessed we've been to always have a skipper

to guide us, when we fall upon our knees.

— Joette McDonald